To My Family

ACKNOWLEDGEMENTS

I wish to thank the publishers of *Commonweal* and *Interpretation: A Journal of Political Philosophy* for allowing me to use passages from my previously published articles on Toynbee. I am also grateful to Houghton Mifflin Company for granting me permission to incorporate some material from chapters I wrote for *Western Civilization: A Concise History*.

TABLE OF CONTENTS

FOREWORD

Arnold Toynbee's life (1889-1975) coincided with the most breath-taking knowledge explosion in human existence. The boundaries of human awareness expanded precipitously in all directions -- into every nook and cranny of inanimate and animate matter, into the structure of the atom and the living cell, into the origins of the universe and human life as well as into the recesses of the human psyche, into ever more sophisticated skills of saving life and destroying it, into the complexities of intense global interdependence. Yet only he among historians let his imagination be fired by that spectacular outburst. Only he can be called a historian truly representative of his time, truly in scale with its enormity. Even the best practitioners of the historical profession (which in these years produced many outstanding scholars) looked the other way, picking partial or even minute aspects of a past that bore little relation to the unprecedented events into which their lives were set. When they talked of historical studies devoted to phenomena of "long duration," they crawled perhaps a yard while Toynbee traversed seven leagues. Only he ventured an all-inclusive perspective covering human existence from the beginnings of recognized civilization down to the formation, during his own lifetime, of an irreversibly interdependent global civilization including all religions, all nations, all surviving previous civilizations despite their diversity or even incompatibility.

One may argue endlessly with Toynbee about detail -- historians have done so with their ant-like, fact-centered intensity. But one cannot deny the exceptional and monumental scope of his work. While his critics still labored on the ground-floor, he matched the astronauts' feat of viewing the earth from the moon, pressing the all-inclusive question: what of the fate of our own civilization? He did so largely on his own and with heroic industry, combining scholarship with analysis and synthesis, writing, as it were, with both hands simultaneously. All the while he kept his vision clear and keen.

Commentators on Toynbee's work have noted its poetic quality. The analogy with poetry is well chosen. The immensity of his subject required an immensely open and concentrated perception nurtured by an inward wholeness that, like poetic inspiration, knows no distinction between intellect, moral sensibility, and spiritual-aesthetic awareness. · Concerned with the fate of civilizations -- specifically his own as it spread over the entire world -- he thought holistically and judgmentally like an Old Testament prophet, painfully conscious of the fragility of civilized life and of the unceasing self-denying spiritual effort necessary to maintain it. In the face of a mind-destroying profusion of data he stuck to the central issues, fully alert to the need for original abstraction and radical synthesis; he appreciated myth and symbol, and above all religion, as conceptually simplifying, civilizing, and community-building essences. In this respect too he was a far greater human being than all his critics who looked at the world through the narrow portholes of a "scientific method" corrupted by the prevailing spiritual shallowness.

Such praise need not deny that Toynbee too had his limitations. In pursuing his grand inquiry he moved into an intellectual *terra incognita* without guidelines or supporting consensus. He worked there with the resources of his cultural tradition and of his times, both of them less universal than he considered them to be yet, everything considered, also comparatively advanced for stretching out historical perspectives to the global scale. Future historians, no doubt, will restructure that inescapable globalism into a meaningful whole with the help of different abstractions and symbols. Yet they cannot do so without the far-sighted capaciousness of mind and perspective that Toynbee developed.

These brief reflections are merely one reader's response to Professor Perry's manuscript. As a guide to the "essential Toynbee" this book will inspire many other responses. It traces the origins

of Toynbee's thought in the aftermath of the first
World War and follows the unfolding of his convictions down to the final Olympian pronouncements on
the condition of contemporary world civilization.
Toynbee's views as they are here presented are perhaps more apt now than they were during his last
years. They certainly need to be read by all open-
minded young historians trying to make sense of
their world -- the whole world -- for themselves as
well as their students and readers. The book will
also assist general readers not only in assessing
one of the great minds of the twentieth century but
also in clarifying their own attitude toward the
world in which they are caught. What could be more
liberating than to rise to the commanding heights
of Toynbee's mind?

                                    Theodore H. Von Laue

PREFACE

Arnold J. Toynbee's *A Study of History* was a deeply felt response to the world wars and totalitarianism that nearly wrecked Western Civilization in the first half of the twentieth century. It was a protest against the materialism and spiritual uneasiness that have pervaded our century; it was a cry of pain by a humane and sensitive thinker who saw the collapse of his Victorian optimism and struggled to comprehend why.

Toynbee made a comparative study of all the world's civilizations, living and dead, analyzing their rise, growth, breakdown, and disintegration. At the core of Toynbee's thought were the convictions that secularism has been a miserable failure, that reason, not guided by spiritual values, is an insufficient integrating principle to sustain civilization, and that tribal-mindedness, which manifests itself in warfare between states, is the principal reason for the breakdown of civilizations. Toynbee considered higher religions to be mankind's greatest achievement and religious prophets humanity's noblest figures. To deal with the ills afflicting the modern world, Toynbee advocated a renewed commitment to the spiritual values of higher religions and the creation of a world-state.

This work is neither a biography of Toynbee nor an analysis of his treatment of the world's civilizations. It is concerned principally with Toynbee's understanding of the nature, meaning, and destiny of Western Civilization.

I am grateful to George Bock for his valuable suggestions.

M.P.

HISTORIAN IN AN AGE OF CRISIS

World War I had a profound impact on the Western mind. Like other intellectuals, Arnold Toynbee, then a promising academic, was disillusioned and demoralized by the war. It left him with the gnawing feeling that Western Civilization had lost its vitality and was caught in the rhythm of breakdown and disintegration. It seemed that Western Civilization too was fragile and perishable, that Western man, despite his extraordinary accomplishments, was never more than a step or two away from barbarism. The orderly, peaceful, and rational world that he had known before the Great War had been shattered. How could one speak of the inviolability of the individual when Europe had become a vast graveyard? Or of the primacy of reason when the nations permitted the slaughter to endure for four years? Or of continuous progress and human perfectibility when civilized men had employed their organizational and technical talents to slaughter millions?

Overwhelmed by the senseless slaughter, Toynbee came to believe that the West was suffering from a profound spiritual crisis. He now felt that Gibbon was wrong in holding that the West could not suffer the same fate as Rome.

> I had continued to concur in Gibbon's judgment till, in the first days of August, 1914, the disaster, unforeseen by me, into which my own world was now rushing, suddenly opened my eyes to the truth. The illumination had caught me in a flash; my illusion that I was the privileged citizen of a stable world had been shattered by a thunderbolt. Since that moment I have seen the world with different eyes and have found that it is not the kind of world that, until then, I had naively imagined it to be.[1]

The shock of the Great War instilled in

Toynbee a profound need to comprehend and confront
the crisis that had afflicted the modern West.
Never had Thucydides seemed more alive and appro-
priate to him. The ancient Greeks had destroyed
themselves by an overzealous attachment to the
city-state; the modern West's devotion to the national state was producing a comparable tragedy.
The system of national states,which many people had
regarded as the source of Europe's greatness,became
for Toynbee the vehicle of the West's decline. The
war also gave Toynbee a sense of mission. Disqual-
ified for military service because of dysentary,
Toynbee would always regard himself as a fortunate
survivor of a conflict that took the lives of half
his classmates. Their deaths would always grieve
him; as a survivor he would always feel that his
declining years were a gift that must be used in
the service of humanity. "The longer I live, the
greater grows my grief and indignation at the wick-
ed cutting short of all those lives. ... The writing of [*A Study of History*] has been one of my responses to the challenge that has been presented
to me by the senseless criminality of human affairs."[2]

Toynbee's thought was a deeply felt response
to the spiritual crisis that afflicted Western Civilization in the twentieth century. Many Europeans
believed that Western Civilization had lost its
vitality and had entered its decline; some, adhering to Spengler's determinism, insisted that the
decline was irreversible and the fall imminent. To
this day it is impossible to escape from the trem-
ors of anxiety that have swept across the West in
the twentieth century. In contrast to nineteenth-
century liberals who spoke glowingly of the future,
twentieth-century intellectuals have been preoccu-
pied with the phenomenon of decay and dissolution.
The crisis is total, as Hans Kohn points out, for
it embraces the West's "intellectual foundations,
its spiritual outlook, its social order, its political forms, and its economic structure. ... This
crisis endangers the survival of that civilization
which seemed so secure in the nineteenth century."[3]

What is the nature of this crisis that caused

many intellectuals, including Toynbee, to lose their Victorian optimism and to contemplate the demise of the West? The crisis may be defined as the Western mind's loss of confidence, and, in some instances, conscious repudiation of the Enlightenment tradition of reason and freedom. The Enlightenment was the intellectual culmination of the trend toward secularism, rationalism, and individualism that had emerged with the breakup of the medieval world-view. In a broad view of Western history, the Enlightenment also represented a harmonizing of a Greek legacy -- a method of perceiving truth, that is, reason -- a Stoic and Roman legacy -- the idea of natural law applicable to all men -- and a Judaeo-Christian legacy -- the belief in human dignity and brotherhood. In 1789 it appeared to both revolutionaries and foreign observers that a new era was dawning that promised to realize the ideals of the Enlightenment: the emancipation of the human personality from superstition and irrational traditions, the triumph of liberty over tyranny, the refashioning of institutions in accordance with reason and justice, the tearing down of barriers to equality. Freedom was man's birthright which would be reclaimed once tyranny and superstition were eliminated; the natural rights of man, hitherto a distant ideal, would now reign on earth, terminating centuries of oppression and misery. Never before had man displayed such confidence in the power of human intelligence to shape the conditions of his existence; never before had the future seemed so replete with hope. In the midst of the French Revolution, Condorcet expressed the hopes of a generation nurtured by the thought of the philosophes:

> The time will therefore come when the sun will shine only on free men who know no other master but their reason; when tyrants and slaves, priests and their stupid or hypocritical instruments will exist only in works of history and on the stage; and when we shall think of them only to pity their victims and their dupes; to maintain ourselves in a state of vigilance by thinking on their excesses; and to

learn how to recognize and so to destroy,
by force of reason, the first seeds of
tyranny and superstition, should they
ever dare to reappear amongst us.[4]

Reason embodied in law, reality planned, shaped,
and governed by the human intellect -- this exalted
conception of human capacities, observed Hegel,
thrilled the world with a spiritual enthusiasm. ·

After the Great War, Paul Valéry summed up the
mood of a generation for whom Condorcet's vision
had lost its power to inspire.

The storm has died away, and still we
are restless, uneasy, as if the storm
were about to break. Almost all the
affairs of men remain in a terrible uncertainty. We think of what has dis-
appeared, we are almost destroyed by
what has been destroyed; we do not know
what will be born, and we fear the
future, not without reason. We hope
vaguely, we dread precisely; our fears
are infinitely more precise than our
hopes; we confess that the charm of
life is behind us ... but doubt and
disorder are in us and with us. There
is no thinking man ... who can hope to
dominate this anxiety, to escape from
this impression of darkness, to measure the probable duration of this
period when the vital relations of
humanity are disturbed profoundly.
... all the fundamentals of our
world have been affected by the war.
... *But among all these injured
things is the Mind*. The Mind has indeed been cruelly wounded; its com-
plaint is heard in the hearts of intellectual men; it passes a mournful
judgment on itself. It doubts itself
profoundly.[5]

Between Condorcet's paean to progress and our
century's testimony of pain, the consciousness of

Europe had been altered. The self-assured confidence in the future gave way to doubt and despair; the unswerving faith in reason was shattered. All of us, like Arthur Koestler, have been "born at the moment when the sun was setting on the Age of Reason."[6] Whereas the philosophes possessed beliefs whose certainty seemed self-evident, the twentieth century is devoid of a unity of outlook; it knows only incoherence, doubt, and confusion. The normative principles, which for the philosophes constituted a standard for political and social reform and a guarantee of human rights, are no longer linked to the natural order. "We certainly no longer believe," says Hannah Arendt, "as the great men of the French Revolution did, in a universal cosmos of which man was a part and whose natural laws he had to imitate and conform to."[7] Dispensing with the belief that there is a natural or rational order from which universal principles can be derived, we no longer hold as self-evident the natural rights of man.

Man's conception of himself has also become problematic. We can no longer define man exclusively in terms of his ability to reason as did Descartes in his famous dictum: "I think therefore I am." Our art, literature, psychology, political behavior all reveal a mysterious underworld of turbulent emotions. The intellect does not seem autonomous, self-regulating, a sovereign master; more often than not it is subject to the rebellious demands of unconscious drives and impulses. Now we cannot escape from the feeling that man's propensity for goodness, his capacity to improve society, his potential for happiness are severely limited by an inherent irrationality, that civilization itself is threatened by our instinctual needs as Freud noted:

> The element of truth behind all this,
> which people are so ready to disavow,
> is that men are not gentle creatures
> who want to be loved and who at the
> most can defend themselves if they are
> attacked; they are, on the contrary,
> creatures among whose instinctual

5

endowments is to be reckoned a powerful
share of aggressiveness. As a result,
their neighbor is for them not only a
potential helper or sexual object, but,
also someone who tempts them to satisfy
their aggressiveness on him,to exploit
his capacity for work without compensa-
tion, to use him sexually without his
consent, to seize his possessions, to
humiliate him, to cause him pain, to
torture and to kill him. *Homo homini
lupus*. ... In consequence of this pri-
mary mutual hostility of human beings,
civilized society is perpetually
threatened with disintegration.[8]

And yet to deny the instinctual, to thwart the non-
rational side of our nature, may lead, as Freud
tells us, to psychic distress, or to a stifling of
our creative capacities, as Nietzsche proclaimed,
or even to a blunting of our moral sentiments, as
Rousseau warned. We cannot have society without
reason and yet man cannot live by reason alone.
Can man provide for intuition and feelings without
undermining the rationality upon which modern civilization rests? Emphasizing the autonomy and uniformity of human beings and the sovereignty of reason, the philosophes were largely untroubled by
this awesome problem.

    This irrational side of human nature, to which
the philosophes had paid scant attention, throws
into confusion the blueprints of philosophers and
social planners. As thinkers doubted, attacked,
and renounced the basic assumptions of the Enlightenment, the West entered into an age of intellectual fragmentation and doubt.

    Along with the diminishing confidence in rea-
son, the twentieth century has seen a loss of faith
in man's capacity to preserve freedom. Even more
distressing, we wonder whether the average person
desires freedom or knows what to do with it. The
enfranchised masses have not been staunch defenders
of political liberty. It seems that without much
reluctance man will trade freedom for security or

national grandeur.   In 1939 John Dewey reflected on this dilemma.

> Does freedom in itself and in the things
> it brings with it seem as important as
> security of livelihood; as food, shelter,
> clothing, or even having a good time? ...
> How do the fruits of liberty compare with
> the enjoyments that spring from a feeling
> of union, of solidarity, with others?
> Will men surrender their liberties if
> they believe that in doing so they will
> obtain the satisfaction that comes from a
> sense of fusion with others and that re-
> spect by others which is the product of
> strength furnished by solidarity?[9]

The paradox of freedom, compellingly stated in Dostoyevski's fable, "The Grand Inquisitor," continues to thwart the best laid plans of liberals. Does freedom of choice plunge the soul into anguish? Is freedom a burden that man cannot tolerate? Will frightened and isolated souls yearn to replace freedom with "miracle, mystery, and authority?" Are the masses far "more satisfied by a doctrine tolerating no other beside itself, than by the granting of liberal freedom,"[10] as Hitler felt?

The crisis of our civilization then is the shattering of the unity of outlook of the Enlightenment and the failure to replace it with another frame of reference. We have lost our spiritual center and are floundering in a sea of uncertainty unable to drop anchor. The crisis of the West is the distressing awareness that reason and freedom, the goals of the philosophes, are fragile and perishable, that the instruments of reason that have expanded man's knowledge of the universe and have given him mastery over nature operate only partially in political and social life, that "the postulate of objectivity has conquered its place in ... men's practice but not in their hearts."[11] It is the feeling that civilization is fighting an unending and, at times, seemingly hopeless battle against the dark forces of the irrational. It is the comprehension that reason has not learned how to provide for the irrational. To crush it by total ratiocination is to deny a fundamental component of human nature to which man cannot submit; to give it full play is to regress into a world of myth in which our modern civilization cannot survive. It is the fear that reason is creating a Frankenstein technology and giant bureaucracies that can depersonalize man and estrange him from himself. It is the painful awareness that while men will fight for freedom, they will also seek to escape from it and will willingly surrender it. It is the recognition that the perfectibility of man and linear progress are only expressions of naive optimism and that our civilization too is mortal.

The crisis of the West is exemplified by the disarray of its intellectuals. Some intellectuals, recognizing the enormity of the crisis, asserted the need to recreate freedom constantly and to salvage respect for reason by enlarging our knowledge of the irrational so that it could be regulated in the interests of civilization. Others, regarding reason as a puny instrument incapable of satisfying man's emotional needs or resolving the problems of industrial society, exalted instincts, drives, feelings. Still others proclaimed that everything is absurd; there is no meaning, only nothingness. Finding a saving faith in fascism, some expressed a hatred for liberal institutions and attitudes, a fascination for violence, and a consuming reverence for the nation.

Overwhelmed by World War I, which took the lives of so many of his contemporaries, and the approach of a second world war, distressed by a ruinous nationalism, a pathological totalitarianism, a paralytic liberalism, and a destructive technology, Toynbee urged mankind to listen to its prophets who have taught the presence of God, the dignity of man, the unity of mankind, and the spiritual purpose of existence. Only by restoring its divine center can Western Civilization rescue itself from crisis. For Toynbee the crisis of Western Civilization was due to its breaking away from Christianity and its unreserved embracing of secularism.

He would agree with Jacques Maritain; "This world was born of Christendom and owes its deepest living strength to the Christian tradition. ... Its ultimate error lay in believing that man is saved by his own stength alone, and that human history is made without God."[12] To one steeped in classical civilization with its notion of overweening pride and retribution and in Christianity which inherited the Hebrew view of history as a conflict between God's law and sinful man, it seemed that world war and totalitarianism were punishments for the West's apostasy from Christianity. Toynbee came to see Western Civilization since the Renaissance moving in the direction of catastrophe.

NOTES

1. Arnold J. Toynbee, *Experiences* (New York: Oxford University Press, 1969), p. 202.

2. Arnold J. Toynbee, *A Study of History*, revised, abridged, illustrated one-volume edition (New York: Oxford University Press and American Heritage Press, 1972), p. 11. Hereafter referred to as *Study*, one-volume edition.

3. Hans Kohn, *Political Ideologies of the Twentieth Century*, 3d. ed., rev. (New York: Harper, 1966), p. 33.

4. Antoine Nicolas de Condorcet, *Sketch for a Historical Picture of the Human Mind*, trans. June Barraclough (London: Weidenfeld & Nicholson, 1955), p. 179.

5. Paul Valéry, *Variety*, trans. Malcolm Cowley (New York: Harcourt, Brace, 1927), pp. 27-28.

6. Cited in Franklin L. Baumer, *Religion and the Rise of Scepticism* (New York: Harcourt, Brace, 1960), p. 187.

7. Cited in Harry S. Kariel, *In Search of Authority* (Glencoe, Illinois: The Free Press, 1964), p. 246.

8. Sigmund Freud, *Civilization and Its Discontents*, trans. James Strachey (New York: W. W. Norton, 1962), pp. 58-59.

9. John Dewey, *Freedom and Culture* (New York: G. P. Putnam's

Sons, 1939), pp. 3-4.

10. Adolf Hitler, *Mein Kampf*, trans. Ralph Manheim (Boston: Houghton Mifflin Co., 1962), p. 42.

11. Jacques Monod, *Chance and Necessity* (New York: Alfred A. Knopf, 1971), p. 170.

12. Jacques Maritain, *Christianity and Democracy* (New York: Scribner's Sons, 1944), p. 21.

HISTORIAN WITH A MISSION

Arnold Toynbee was born in 1889, the son of Harry Toynbee, a social worker, and Sarah Marshall Toynbee, one of the first women in England to receive a college degree. His interest in history was prompted by his mother, who was an historian, and by his great-uncle, a sea captain, whose stories about voyages to the East excited the young Toynbee. Toynbee attended boarding school at Winchester where he cultivated "the classics with an almost demonic fervor,"[1] reading, composing, and translating beyond the requirements of the demanding curriculum. He won a classical scholarship and entered Oxford in 1907. After completing his studies, he received a fellowship to teach ancient history at his college, Balliol. Before assuming his duties at Balliol, Toynbee spent the academic year 1911-1912 hiking, primarily in the Greek countryside, an experience that intensified his feelings for the Graeco-Roman world which had become his spiritual home as a result of his classical education.

From Graeco-Roman civilization Toynbee acquired a model by which to measure the rise, growth, and decline of all the world's civilizations. From the Bible, which he also studied in great depth, Toynbee learned to look for a religious meaning behind the facts of history; history is the unfolding of a divine plan. Thus from youth Toynbee was steeped in the outlook and values of Hellenism and Christianity the two traditions that are the foundation of Western Civilization. Like Thomas Aquinas, Toynbee would seek a creative synthesis between the rationalism of Athens and the revelation of Jerusalem.

In 1915 Toynbee left Oxford to work for the Political Intelligence Department of the Foreign Office and in 1919 served as a member of the British delegation at the Paris Peace Conference. From 1919 to 1924 he held a chair in Byzantine and modern Greek studies in the University of London. In 1924 he was invited by Chatham House to launch the annual *Survey of International Affairs*.

Toynbee conceived *A Study of History* in 1921 and began writing in 1927. Volumes 1-3 were published in 1934, volumes 4-6 in 1939, volumes 7-10 in 1951, volume 11, an historical atlas and gazetteer, in 1959, and volume 12, a reconsideration of his theories and a discussion of the views of his critics, in 1961. Remarkably, from 1924 to 1956 Toynbee also wrote or edited the annual *Survey of International Affairs*. Toynbee confessed that he would have been conscience stricken and unhappy if he had slackened in his work. But it was more than a work ethic that drove him to devote himself to *A Study of History*. The impulse behind this monumental effort was a deeply felt need to be of service to humanity.

In *A Study of History* Toynbee listed 21 (later 26) civilizations, living and dead, and examined their rise, growth, breakdown, and disintegration, always, in the process, searching for valid patterns that apply to civilization in general. Toynbee demonstrated immense learning and research, ranging over the histories of ancient Mesopotamia and Egypt, Greece and Rome, Byzantium and Islam, China and India, the Americas and Polynesia.

The first six volumes were written with the memory of World War I still strong and when it appeared that the worn out Western democracies might well succumb to one of two dynamic totalitarian ideologies. That the modern West could give rise to World War I and totalitarianism convinced Toynbee that Western Civilization was now far into its Time of Troubles. In volumes 7-10, written in the aftermath of Hiroshima and in the early stages of the Cold War, Toynbee still had doubts about the vitality of the West and its ability to escape from the rhythm of breakdown and disintegration that had ruined other civilizations. However, in these later volumes, Toynbee emerged more and more as a prophet of world integration, a theme that was expanded in his writings of the 1960's and 1970's.

Toynbee's goal was a world-state dedicated to achieving peace and social justice.

SYNTHESIS AND UNIVERSALISM

Toynbee insisted that it was the duty of the historian to search for the larger meaning of history. History must be more than fact finding; the historian must be more than an antiquarian who collects data encyclopaedicaly and shapelessly; he must be more than a specialist who divides human affairs into numerous and minute morsels. From his classical education Toynbee derived the conviction that human affairs are intelligible only when viewed comprehensively. As a student of the classics, he learned to view the literature, art, philosophy, politics, and history of antiquity not as isolated subjects but as facets of a distinct world-view. To be understood properly, they must be seen as expressions of a humanist outlook that pervaded Greek civilization. Among the modern historians that inspired Toynbee were Gibbon, Freeman, Bury, and Mommsen, for each of them was motivated by a comprehensive-mindedness. This need for synthesis led Toynbee to reject national histories as too parochial. In order to comprehend English history, for example, it is necessary to examine it within the context of the broader field of Western Civilization. Toynbee would study nothing less than an entire civilization.

Toynbee's approach to history was also universal, for ultimately the boundaries of his investigation encompassed all the world's civilizations, surviving and extinct. To comprehend the historical forces that cause a civilization to grow and to decline, it is necessary, said Toynbee, to compare the histories of various civilizations. Such comparisons permit the historian to discern general principles and patterns that are common to all civilizations. To study all the world's civilizations and to give form to the great variety of human history -- could there be a more ambitious and demanding task?

13

By eschewing specialization in preference to comprehensiveness, Toynbee's *Study* is vulnerable to criticism by specialists who have mastered small segments of history and can detect errors which an enterprise of this scope must contain. Nevertheless, this does not negate Toynbee's achievement. The true importance of the *Study* is that it challenges historians to think critically about broad themes in history, about patterns in human affairs; it forces the analytic historian to transcend his special area of professional interest and to deal with the larger meaning of the human experience. From the vantage point of a Toynbee-like history, says William H. McNeill,

> New insights may arise with breadth of view; fallible and never completely provable perhaps, yet enormously stimulating to exact and careful study which may find new questions to ask of familiar data in the light of general ideas generated by men like Toynbee. No multiplication of specialisms or narrowing down of fields of history in the interest of more perfect accuracy can by itself hope to achieve such an enrichment of our understanding of man's past. Interaction between large views, bold hypothesis, fallible intuitions, and exact, detailed scholarship is what we need. If we concentrate upon the latter alone, by drawing ever closer to the facts and seeing details ever more completely, we may blind ourselves to other aspects of reality.[2]

Toynbee's decision to study world history showed his debt to Polybius from whom he acquired "a universal view of history which has interested me all my life."[3] Polybius sought to explain Rome's march to world empire by examining history on a grand scale. He said that it was impossible to understand the reduction of the Mediterranean world to Roman power by writing isolated narratives of Roman activities in Spain or Sicily; Roman history must be examined on a universal scale.

Polybius' history linked together the affairs of Italy, Greece, Africa, and Asia, giving expression to the universalism and cosmopolitanism of the Hellenistic Age.

But the principal source of Toynbee's universalism was religion. Adapting the thought of the prophets of higher religions, who have taught that as God is one so too should there be the unity of mankind, Toynbee, held that mankind is one family in the making. A universal history accorded with Toynbee's sense of mission. He hoped that such a history would contribute to the world-mindedness which he considered a precondition for man's self-preservation; mankind must become one family, he said, or it will destroy itself.

Toynbee's world-mindedness demonstrated a humanitarianism and tolerance which, said Hans Kohn, resembles that of Tolstoy, Schweitzer, and Lessing. Like Lessing, Toynbee held that actions and an ethical spirit matter more than dogma. "As Lessing saw in Judaism, Christianity, and Islam variations on a single theme, so Mr. Toynbee ... sees all universal religions ... as equally sharing in their great message to mankind, the message of unity beyond all ethnic divisions."[4]

For Toynbee history was a calling. He felt that all creative effort was ultimately barren if it did not enhance man's spiritual and social development, if it did not promote harmony and eliminate discord. Toynbee, who considered himself a survivor of World War I, felt a profound need to help his fellow man. He believed that in a world struggling for survival, he had an obligation to make a contribution to the understanding of the nature of the crisis that had afflicted the West and now the entire globe and to offer remedies.

Thus Toynbee wrote history didactically; he believed that from his study of the past he had gained certain insights into the human condition that could assist a foundering humanity. While historical precedents are not scientific blueprints, said Toynbee, they do allow man to understand better and to cope more successfully with contemporary problems.

While maintaining that there were patterns to the past, Toynbee rejected determinism. He did not hold that past occurrences were inevitable or that out of necessity the patterns of the past will repeat themselves in the future. Toynbee first read Spengler's *Decline of the West* in 1920. He approved of Spengler's inquiring into the histories of whole societies, instead of national states, and of his comparative approach to the study of civilizations. He also employed Spengler's thesis that there are patterns to the growth and decay of civilizations. What he disliked about Spengler was his determinism, his "arbitrary fiat," his dogmatic insistence that "civilization arose, developed, declined, and foundered in unvarying conformity with a fixed timetable."[5] Unlike Spengler, Toynbee believed that despite our knowledge of the past we cannot predict with any certainty the course of history; human affairs are amenable to regularities, but these "laws" are not inexorable. The repetitive element in history does not make man a slave to fate but provides him with an opportunity for creative action; to a large extent man can shape his own destiny. For Spengler, civilizations were organic bodies that are destroyed by necessity; rejecting the organic model, Toynbee attributed decline to man's own nature which he has the capacity to remedy. Nor is man a helpless prisoner of the past; he has it in his power to break with self-destructive traditions and practices, but this requires a mighty effort. Toynbee insisted that he was not a determinist. History reveals recurrent patterns but there is no inevitability; man has the freedom to shape his future.

For Toynbee, man achieves freedom through self-mastery and self-determination, when he is able to break with tradition, overcome habit, and meet new challenges. The highest form of freedom, said Toynbee, is spiritual growth; when man guides his conduct according to God's values he has successfully responded to the greatest challenge of all -- that presented by his own nature. Man thereby demonstrates he has freedom of choice. In rejecting God's law of love, man brings about his own disaster; he is overwhelmed by the irrationality, greed, and aggressiveness inherent in human nature. Freedom requires continuous acts of creation, for man must always transcend the limitations posed by human nature. In doing so, he not only performs an act of self-transfiguration that brings him closer to God, he also acquires the capacity to improve society.

CIVILIZATION: RISE, GROWTH, BREAKDOWN, DISINTEGRATION

Much of *A Study of History* deals with an analysis of the rise, growth, breakdown, and disintegration of civilizations. For most of human history, said Toynbee, man lived in primitive societies in which the younger generation acquired its outlook and habits by imitating its dead ancestors. A society ruled by custom remains static. The breakthrough to civilization came when creative personalities broke with tradition and attracted the following of the uncreative majority. The impulse that gave rise to civilization, stemmed neither from any special quality of race or from a favorable environment, but from a creative response to a challenge. The founders of Egyptian and Mesopotamian civilizations were heroic pioneers who made marsh lands give way to irrigation works, fields, and cities.

In *challenge-and-response*, Toynbee had a plausible explanation to account for the rise, growth, and decline of civilization. In accounting for the origin of civilization, Toynbee stressed not the environment in and of itself but the "human heroism" that enabled man to transform the environment for his own benefit. In the Nile valley man had to clear jungles and drain swamps before he could plant; he had to subdue and order the wantonness and formlessness of nature before he could create civilization. This point is central to Toynbee's analysis of civilizations. Man's great achievements stem from creative acts of the human spirit; conversely, spiritual and psychological defects ultimately cause a civilization's decline. Hence, for Toynbee, the essential problem confronting the modern West is not material but spiritual.

Man, said Toynbee, achieved a *tour de force* when he overcame physical and human challenges and created civilization. But if a civilization is to grow, it must move from "challenge through response to further challenge."[6] The creative spirit that enabled a civilization to rise must be preserved if the civilization is to avoid arrest and to continue its growth. A society in growth progresses toward self-determination, that is, it provides itself with fresh challenges that trigger a chain reaction of successful responses and still further challenges enabling it to move from strength to strength. It possesses an *élan vital*, an inner spiritual power, which enables it to face successfully one challenge after another.

It is creative personalities, men who "have succeeded in attaining self-determination through self-mastery,"[7] that propel humanity out of its inertia and enable a society to grow. Toynbee agreed with Bergson who held that "It is only the thrust of genius that has ever forced the inertia of Humanity to yield."[8] These pioneers break with custom, stir the inert and uncreative majority to follow their lead, and keep civilization in a healthy state of dynamic movement.

Growth for Toynbee stems from creative personalities who gain the mimesis of ordinary human beings. But when leadership fails, self-determination is lost and the harmony that society had shown during its period of growth ends. The once creative minority becomes impotent and cannot cope successfully with new challenges. During such times, the great mass of people, for whom civilization is only a thin veneer, revert back to their primitive humanity and society is in danger of breaking down.

Societies are not predestined to death, insisted Toynbee. Civilizations are not condemned by fate or by forces outside human control. Nor is breakdown the consequence of a mortal blow delivered by invading armies. Rather, civilizations break down for internal reasons, from wounds that are self-inflicted. "The most that the alien enemy has achieved has been to give the expiring suicide his *coup de grace* or to devour his carcass after it has already become carrion."[9] The truth is, as George Meredith said: "We are betrayed by what is false within." Suicide, not murder, is the reason why civilizations die. Civilizations break down when there is a deterioration within the social order, an inability to respond to challenges, and a subsequent loss of that self-determination that had once impelled growth; instead of variety and versatility, there is deadening uniformity and un-inventiveness.

One aspect of the process of breakdown is "resting on one's oars." Becoming infatuated with its own achievement, a creative minority looks to the past, becomes senile, and loses the *élan* that had once enabled it to respond creatively to challenges. Resting on one's oars may take the form of idolizing an institution that has outlived its usefulness, as was the case with the Greeks whose infatuation with the polis eventually thwarted creativity; it prevented them from achieving the unity that alone could save Hellenic civilization from the suicidalness of internecine warfare.

Societies on the downhill slide from breakdown to disintegration, said Toynbee, are torn by social discord operating on two levels. First there is warfare among a number of parochial states within the same society until a single state delivers a knockout blow and creates a universal state. But a universal state established through violence, as in the case of Rome, cannot breathe new life into a disintegrating civilization. It can only provide a temporary reprieve.

Secondly, a disintegrating society breaks up into a dominant minority, an internal proletariat, and an external proletariat (barbarian warrior bands). The common consciousness that had bound together the different ranks of society during the civilization's growth falls apart. The creative minority that had once spurred the society to grow, loses its ability to create and becomes merely a dominant minority that "attempts to hold by force -- against all right and reason -- a position of inherited privilege which it has ceased to merit,"[10] and the internal proletariat, responding to the deterioration of the creative minority, executes its act of secession. The proletariat, feeling disinherited and unwanted, no longer follows a dominant minority that has lost its capacity for leadership.

This schism in the body social of a disintegrating society is the outward expression of a spiritual rift in human souls. In such a society human behavior and feelings are in turmoil. Some people demonstrate a loss of the creative faculty by giving free reign to their appetites; others go to the opposite extreme and become ascetics. A selfish individualism replaces a sense of duty to the community. Another conspicuous attitude of mind displayed by individuals living in disintegrating societies is the "hopeless feeling of being adrift in an uncontrollable, if not evil, Universe."[11] The sense of spiritual uncertainty leads many to find comfort by glorifying an earlier period of time (archaism) or by dreaming up utopias (futurism). Both archaism and futurism are signs of defeatism and therefore are uncreative responses to the spiritual crisis. The dominant minority in a disintegrating civilization adopts the cultural patterns of the proletariat; this results in a vulgarization of art, literature, and manners.

The dominant minority, resting on its oars, becomes rigid and ineffectual. Nevertheless it performs an act of creativity -- the establishment of a universal state. A universal state, according to Toynbee's scheme, emerges *after* a civilization has already begun to break down; it is the means by which the dominant minority checks for a time the process of disintegration. The universal state does not represent recovery from a Time of Troubles that might be centuries old; it is only a rally that enables the afflicted society "to enjoy a brief 'Indian Summer' before its final dissolution."[12] When the universal state comes too late and at too great a cost it will not endure, despite the expectations of its citizens who believe their earthly commonwealth is really immortal. However long it may last, it represents only the last phase of a civilization prior to its extinction.

For Toynbee, the ultimate significance of the universal state is that it provides a setting within which a universal church can grow in its tender infancy. But the universal state belongs wholly to the past. So too do the bevy of barbarian warrior bands that sprout on the universal state's borders. It is the universal church created by the seceding proletariat that will become the predominant force shaping the future.

The breakdown of a civilization makes possible a spiritual advance -- the emergence of a higher religion. A civilization fulfills its destiny when it ministers to the birth of a higher religion. Religion was at the core of Toynbee's historical consciousness. It provided him with a framework for assessing the essential meaning of Western Civilization and for explaining its near collapse in the twentieth century.

THE PRIMACY OF RELIGION

Toynbee maintained that in studying history as a whole we should "relegate economic and political history to a subordinate place and give religious history primacy. For religion, after all, is the serious business of the human race."[13] For Toynbee, the vocation of historian is a calling of a very special nature. It is "a call from God to feel after Him and find Him. ... History [is] a vision -- dim and partial ... of God revealing Himself in actions to souls that were sincerely seeking Him."[14] It leads us to a revelation of God and a hope of communion with Him. Toynbee believed that his craft was "ultimately a quest for the vision of God at work in History."[15] The facts of history, he maintained, are "clues to the nature and meaning of

the mysterious Universe and our place in it. ...
The spiritual reality behind the phenomena is, I
believe, the ultimate objective of all curiosity."[16]
This religious feeling pervaded Toynbee's historical consciousness.

Toynbee's view of history derived in part from
the biblical conception that it is through history
that man's will clashes with God's commands. God
showed man the way to righteousness, but man also
has the freedom to defy God. While God's hand was
at work in history, it was man who essentially made
his own history, for God's punishments were something that stubborn and rebellious man brought upon
himself. Thus for Toynbee history is filled with
spiritual meaning; it is a theodicy in which progress is measured by man's awareness of God.

Toynbee's conception of human nature was in-
separable from his religious outlook. Inherent in
human nature, he said, is "a vein of diabolical
evil," that manifests itself on an individual level
in self-centeredness and on the social level in
warfare and class antagonisms which have proved
fatal to civilization. Toynbee regarded as naive
the liberal belief in the essential goodness of
man; for him the atrocities of the twentieth century were sufficient proof of man's capacity for
evil. But Toynbee also believed that human nature
has an inherent capacity for goodness. In every
human soul a struggle is waged between these two
irreconcilable spiritual forces. This spiritual
division of the soul, said Toynbee, manifests itself in human society which is an arena of continual
warfare between good and evil. Human nature is out
of balance, said Toynbee. Man has demonstrated a
much greater talent for mastering inanimate nature
than for controlling his own emotions and for living in fellowship with others. If the individual
and society are not to be consumed by wickedness,
man must seek the support of higher religions --
Christianity, Islam, Judaism, Buddhism, Hinduism,
Zoroastrianism. Every human being, said Toynbee,
is disposed to behave as if he were the center of
the universe and to exploit everyone else in the
universe. The higher religions have tried to help

the individual to overcome an inherent self-centeredness and the community a destructive tribal-
mindedness. As the center of human existence becomes the love of a Supreme Being, man treats his
fellows with consideration and respect.

It was not a commitment to a particular theology that drew Toynbee to religion but an attachment
to prophetic values. Higher religions, he believed,
enable the individual to find a purpose in life and
to deal with emotional distress; they promote better relations among human beings and facilitate social welfare. Belief in God makes the individual a
better person and instills a social conscience in
society. Only the values of higher religions can
rescue man from a dehumanizing technology and totalitarianism; only prophetic values can prevent
humanity from destroying itself in a nuclear holo-
caust.

Toynbee defined religion as a "human being's
relation to an ultimate reality behind and beyond
the phenomena of the Universe in which each of us
awakes to consciousness."[17] Convinced that there
exists a spiritual element within human nature,
Toynbee then inferred the existence of an ultimate
reality with which this spiritual element seeks
communion, although he recognized that the existence of an ultimate reality is unverifiable.

Man has always demonstrated religious feelings, declared Toynbee, for it is through religion
that he has tried to answer questions about the
purpose of existence and the meaning of death.
Toynbee classified the varieties of religions into
three categories -- the worship of nature, the worship of man, and the worship of Absolute Reality,
that is God. Primitive man expressed his religious
feelings through the worship of nature -- animals,
rain, moon, stars. Nature gods were for primitive
man embodiments of the presence behind nature of
forces to which he was at mercy. Nature worship
receded, said Toynbee, because man had begun to exercise power over nature; man does not deify things
that he has learned to control. While the primitive religion of nature worship persisted after the

rise of civilization, it was eventually superseded
by another lower religion -- the deification of a
human being (the god-like ruler) or a human institution (the sacrosanct state). In Greece, for example, the Greek goddess Athena, originally a nature divinity, came to represent the political
power of the human community, Athens. In idolizing
the collective power of their community, asserted
Toynbee, the Athenians still embraced a lower religion. By giving total commitment to their city,
the Greeks unleashed the dark side of human nature,
massacring and enslaving for their deified community. This transformation of the human community
into a virtual god lead to wars that ultimately
wrecked Hellenic civilization.

Toynbee defined the period from the eighth
century B.C. to the seventh century A.D. as an age
of spiritual progress. It began with the Hebrew
prophets and ended with Mohammed. Included within
the period were others of the world's great religious prophets: Buddha, Lao-tze, Confucious, Zara-
thustra, Socrates. Toynbee continually urged man
to return to the values taught by these prophets,
history's most inspired men. The higher religions,
insisted Toynbee, have given man the cure for his
spiritual malady; they have shown him how he can
transcend greed and aggressiveness and improve the
quality of social relationships. The higher religions have taught that man is not God, that human
power is limited, that love is the greatest good,
that man should never deify a human being or a human institution.

The human psyche, said Toynbee, will resist
all efforts of reason to eliminate religious sentiments; if the feelings are not directed toward the
higher religions, they will find other outlets, for
human beings cannot be without some form of religion. If the mind is not restrained and elevated
by higher religions, it will embrace myths that
give vent to the worst elements of human nature.
For Toynbee, the most dangerous expression of mythical thinking is the deification of the parochial
community (nationalism) which he saw as a principal
reason for the breakdown of civilizations.

Toynbee's conception of religion was personal rather than sectarian. Reared as an Anglican, Toynbee became an agnostic while an undergraduate at Oxford, concluding "that religion itself was an unimportant illusion."[18] Later, no doubt under the influence of the Great War, the rise of totalitarianism, and an impending second world war, he attributed an inestimable value to higher religions: they help man to overcome depression and anxiety, to conquer his destructive self-centeredness, and to assure him that in spite of his sinfulness he is redeemable.

While Toynbee admired the spiritual message of the higher religions, he rejected doctrines that lacked credibility. For example, he could not adhere to some essential Christian dogmas -- the Virgin Birth, the Resurrection, the Ascension -- for they are irreconcilable with what science tells us about the uniformity of nature. Nor did he regard Jesus as divine, but as a man inspired by a love of humanity unmatched by any other human being. To this extent, of all of God's children, Jesus came closest to fulfilling the ideals of the sonship of God. What is most valuable in Christianity is its precept that "self-sacrificing love is the most powerful of all the spiritual impulses known to us."[19]

While Christianity occupied a central place in Toynbee's thought, he came to believe that it was not a unique and final revelation. All the higher religions are alternate approaches to the mystery of existence. All the higher religions are variations on a theme; they all present some facet of God's truth. They all aspire to help the individual to attain the true end of life -- communion with a higher spiritual reality. They all liberate man by teaching that God alone, not man or his creations, is the supreme value in the universe and that only He is worthy of worship. They all help men and women to deal with life's misfortunes. They all hold the promise of salvation, a need which human beings feel more compellingly than the need for truth. They all help man to combat egocentricity and social discord. By addressing themselves to all mankind, not just a part of it, the higher religions enable man to overcome barriers between states and civilizations. The higher religions were revolutionary new departures for they all proclaimed a message of universalism -- the unity of mankind, a condition that Toynbee considered necessary for human survival.

Toynbee did not regard himself as an orthodox member of any of the higher religions, because he could not accept their exact and definitive answers to the riddle of existence, but he subscribed to their spiritual values -- love and compassion. Favoring "the maximum of religion with the minimum of dogma,"[20] he wanted all the historic higher religions to separate the essentials of their faith, a love of God and therefore a love of man, from doctrinal and ritual accretions.

He criticized religion's efforts to resist scientific truth by claiming authority "over other provinces of knowledge which were really Reason's legitimate domain."[21] While religion cannot compete with science in the attempt to understand and manipulate nature, science cannot provide answers to the most crucial questions of life -- man's relationship to himself, his fellows, and his God. For such spiritual insight, said Toynbee, we must turn to the higher religions.

Toynbee was a religious moralist who found rationalism intrinsically imperfect, incomplete and inadequate, and secularism a miserable failure. What gives unity to his thought is its spirituality and universalism -- a vision of the community of man united by a love of God. He held steadfastly that the Western liberal-rational tradition simply cannot bind men together in peace and fellowship, for it cannot permanently restrain man's evil nature which manifests itself in wars among peoples and in conflicts between classes. To be effective, liberalism and rationalism must draw inspiration from prophetic values. The inspiration of the Gospels must radiate widely into temporal society. For Toynbee, Christianity constitutes more than divine truth propagated by churches and structured by theologians. It is an historic force that is woven into the fabric of our existence; its values improve individual life and the social order.

But Toynbee was no simple-minded devotee. While displeased with the secularism of the modern West, he would not betray the heritage of intellectual freedom bequeathed by the Scientific Revolution and the Enlightenment. He would attempt to fashion a synthesis of reason and religion to fit the requirements of the modern age.

METHODOLOGY

Toynbee's historiography was a peculiar mixture of empiricism and mythical thinking. In the tradition of nineteenth-century positivists, particularly Buckler, Toynbee collected facts and statistics and searched for general rules and laws that govern human affairs. Toynbee felt that this empiricism distinguished his work from Spengler's. While Toynbee maintained that his method of inquiry was empirical, his critics have insisted that facts were forced to fit an arbitrary and rigid *a priori* framework. He tried to validate empirically preconceptions to which he had already committed himself. Consequently, said McNeill, "in the interest of fitting data into a pattern, he sometimes seems to cut and slice reality in an arbitrary and even fantastic fashion."[22] What Toynbee held to be logical conclusions deduced dispassionately from the facts were really personal value judgments and the facts themselves were often arbitrarily selected.

Moreover, much of Toynbee's history derived from mythology which Toynbee found a valuable assistance to the historian. From mythology Toynbee hoped to obtain an intuitive grasp of what is most essential to the human condition; he held that mythology expressed universal truths in a unique way. While the insights derived from mythological analogy are unverifiable, "mythology has a wider reach than science and a deeper penetrative power;"[23] it is a means of apprehending and expressing universal truth. By means of mythological analogy "the range of human intuition and understanding," could be extended "beyond the limits of the knowledge attainable through logical processes of thought."[24] For this reason he would drive "science and mythology in double harnass. ... the two steeds, side by side, can carry us farther than either steed can by itself."[25] It is from Plato, said Toynbee, that he acquired this approach.

> Plato taught me, by example, not to be ashamed of using my imagination as well as my intellect. He taught me, when, in a mental voyage, I found myself at the upper limit of the atmosphere accessible to the Reason, not to hesitate to let my imagination carry me on up into the stratosphere on the wings of a myth. In never being either too proud or too timid to take a myth for the sake of reconnoitering regions of the Spiritual Universe beyond Reason's range, Plato was showing both the humility and the audacity of a great mind. ... I have now lived to see the subconscious well-spring of Poetry and Prophecy restored to honor in the Western World by the genius of C.G. Jung.[26]

Like Plato, Toynbee relied on sudden flashes of insight and resorted to myth and metaphor to make a crucial point. To elucidate his theory of the rise, growth, and demise of civilization, he summoned Goethe, Milton, Aeschylus, and the Bible. Plato held that underlying the multiplicity of phenomena were principles of unity; Toynbee, Plato's disciple, also assumed that beneath the multifariousness of historical experience lie principles of order. There is form to the historical process.

Toynbee was also greatly indebted to Bergson whose works he avidly read during his student days and to whom he often referred. Originally attracted to positivism, Bergson turned away from the positivist claim that science could explain everything and fulfill all human needs. Such an emphasis on the intellect, said Bergson, sacrifices spiritual

28

impulses, imagination, and intuition and reduces the soul to a mere mechanism. The methods of science cannot reveal ultimate, reality, Bergson insisted. European civilization must recognize the limitations of scientific rationalism. The method of intuition, whereby the mind strives for an immanent relationship with the object, becoming one with it, can tell us more about reality than the method of analysis used by science. Entering into the object through an intuitive experience is the avenue to a truth that the calculations and measurements of science cannot obtain. Although not based upon scientific procedures, insisted Bergson, the method of intuition is a superior avenue to knowledge. Science is not the only avenue to truth and the mind is not a collection of atoms operating according to mechanical principles but a stream of consciousness with extraordinary intuitive capacities. Bergson's philosophy pointed away from science toward religious mysticism.

Like Bergson, Toynbee had a deep impulse to comprehend life directly and totally and toward this end he gave validity to extra-scientific knowledge. Like Bergson, Toynbee sought to complement the intellect with intuition, thereby arriving at a more complete understanding of personality and life. Also like Bergson, he yearned for communion with a transcendent reality of higher values and demonstrated some of the qualities of a religious mystic. Toynbee agreed with Bergson that men can never overcome their primitive tribalism and progress to ecumenical concord unless they demonstrate a common allegiance to God.

It is precisely this approach that aroused the ire of professional historians and made suspect Toynbee's claim that his conclusions were based upon an empirical study. Repelled by his religious-mythical orientation, many critics accused Toynbee of distorting the truth, undermining rationalism, and regressing to myth. "He is a man who believes ... in a strange mysticism about history. ... His is not the talent of science but of belief,"[27] said Ortega y Gasset. "For although Toynbee, in analyzing civilizations, claims to be dispassionate and scientific, in fact his whole analysis is governed by strong emotional prejudice,"[28] said H.R. Trevor-Roper. This is quite understandable, for professional historians are generally hostile to a religious world-view and are discomforted by religious explanations for social problems, especially when written in exalted tones and supported by long passages from the Bible, St. Augustine, Bishop Bossuet, and Bergson. Like G. J. Reiner, they are scornful of a methodology that uses myths and metaphors "not merely for the purpose of assisting thought, but as the basis for subsequent reasoning and classification. ... I dislike Toynbee's method, because it dwells in the sphere of myth and allegory, outside rationality."[29] Toynbee maintained that he aimed "to try out the scientific approach to human affairs and to test how far it will carry us,"[30] but ultimately he was a mythical thinker whose historical outlook was permeated with religious hopes and feeling. He praised Ibn Khaldun's *Universal History* "for bursting the bounds of this world and breaking through into an Other World," and St. Augustine's *City of God* for showing him "the tradition in which these two worlds stand to one another."[31] This attitude of mind repels both the professional historian and the liberal humanist. Critics agreed essentially with Pieter Geyl's assessment of Toynbee: "The problems ... which ... have to do with the health and prospects of survival of a civilization have always been tackled and will always be tackled on a different plane from that of religion."[32] Many of Toynbee's passages that seem to preach against the pagans offend the liberal-rationalist temperament; his pleas for spirituality and his analysis in religious terms of the ills of modern society are reminiscent of St. Augustine to whom humanists do not turn for inspiration or guidance. There are numerous parallels between the *City of God*, written when Rome was dying, and *A Study of History*, written when the West seemed near collapse. Like Augustine, Toynbee measured progress by spiritual advances -- man moving closer to God -- and held that doing without God ends in the undoing of man. Much of Augustinian pessimism pervades Toynbee's work. Most repulsive to liberal humanists was Toynbee's view that a civilization fulfills its historical mission by giving rise to a higher religion, that history is a progressive process with communion with God as the ultimate goal.

Toynbee's religious orientation provided him with a framework for comprehending the major stages of Western Civilization and for explaining the West's near collapse in the twentieth century. For Toynbee, Hellenism, the parent of the West, failed because it overvalued man and his creations. Hellenism's collapse prepared the way for a spiritual advance -- the Christian Middle Ages; the disintegration of medieval religious unity and the transformation of the West into a post-Christian civilization set the wheels of decline in motion.

NOTES

1. *Experiences*, p. 14.

2. William H. McNeill, "Some Basic Assumptions of Toynbee's *A Study of History*," in Edward T. Gargan, ed., *The Intent of Toynbee's History* (Chicago: Loyola University Press, 1961), pp. 31-32.

3. *Toynbee on Toynbee: A Conversation Between Arnold J. Toynbee and G. R. Urban* (New York: Oxford University Press, 1974), p. 16.

4. Hans Kohn, *Political Ideologies of the Twentieth Century*, pp. 269-70.

5. Arnold J. Toynbee, *Civilization on Trial* (New York: Oxford University Press, 1948; reprint edition published together with *The World and the West* (Cleveland: World, 1958), p. 20.

6. Arnold J. Toynbee, *A Study of History*, 12 vols. (New York: Oxford University Press, 1962-1964), 3: 128. The citation refers to the paperback edition. Volumes 1-3 were originally published in 1934, volumes 4-6 in 1939, volumes 7-10 in 1954, volume 11, an historical atlas and gazetteer, in 1959, and volume 12, a reconsideration of his theories and a discussion of his critics, in 1961. All references are to the paperback edition henceforth referred to as *Study*.

7. *Ibid.*, p. 234.

8. *Ibid.*, p. 237.

9. *Study*, 4: 115.

10. *Study*, 5: 26.

11. *Study*, one-volume edition, p. 243.

12. *Ibid.*, p. 228.

13. Arnold J. Toynbee, *Civilization on Trial*, p. 89.

14. *Study*, 10: 1.

15. *Study*, 10: 42.

16. *Experiences*, p. 90.

17. *Ibid.*, p. 125.

18. *Ibid.*, p. 127.

19. *Ibid.*, p. 135.

20. *Ibid.*, p. 143.

21. *Study*, 7b: 476.

22. Gargan, ed., *The Intent of Toynbee's History*, p. 41.

23. *Study*, 12: 40.

24. *Ibid.*, p. 250.

25. *Ibid.*, p. 40.

26. *Study*, 10: 228.

27. José Ortega y Gasset, *An Interpretation of Universal History*, trans. Mildred Adams (New York: W. W. Norton, 1975), pp. 251-52.

28. H. R. Trevor-Roper, "Arnold Toynbee's Millenium," *Encounter* (June 1957), reprinted in *Historical Essays*

(New York: Harper, 1957), p. 300.

29. G. J. Reiner, *History: Its Purpose and Method*, excerpted in Montagu, ed., *Toynbee and History*, pp. 74-75.

30. Toynbee, "What I am Trying to Do," in Montagu, *Toynbee and History*, p. 6.

31. *Study*, 10: 236.

32. Pieter Geyl, *Debates With Historians* (New York: The New American Library, 1958), p. 159.

HELLENISM AND CHRISTIANITY

Western Civilization is a confluence of two
traditions -- Graeco-Roman and Judaeo-Christian.
Toynbee's interpretation of these traditions is
crucial to an understanding of his philosophy of
history and his interpretation of the modern West.

HELLENISM

"Had Greek civilization never existed," said
the poet W. H. Auden, "we would never have become
fully conscious, which is to say that we would
never have become, for better or worse, fully human."[1] Breaking with the mythopoeic outlook of the
Near East, the Greeks conceived a world-view whose
focus was not mythic gods or priest-kings but man.
In Greece there arose a new conception of nature as
orderly and intelligible to reason and a new conception of the human being -- his capacity for rational thought, his need for freedom, his worth as
an individual.

In maintaining that nature does not behave
haphazardly, that it is not governed by blind
chance, that it is not manipulated by arbitrary and
willful gods, but proceeds according to general
laws, early Greek philosophers initiated the movement from myth to reason that came to characterize
every level of Greek cultural life by the age of
Pericles. From a rational inquiry into nature, the
Greek philosophical spirit turned to a rational investigation of man and the human community. Here
the decisive figure was Socrates who insisted that
man use his reason to make sense out of his own
life. Through reason the individual gains knowledge of ethical values and takes control of his
own life. Moral norms are not revealed to man in
the form of divine commandments, but must be dis-
covered by the individual himself through critical
analysis. Socrates wanted to subject all human beliefs and behavior to the clear light of reason;

in this way ethics would be removed from the realm of authority, dogma, superstition, and myth.

The Greeks were the first to define man by his capacity to reason. It was the great achievement of the Greek spirit to rise above magic, mystery, authority, and custom and to discover the means of giving order to nature and society. Every feature of Greek civilization -- science, philosophy, art, literature, politics, writing of history -- shows a growing reliance upon human reason and a diminishing dependence upon divine guidance.

Political freedom also originated in Greece. In Mesopotamia and Egypt man had no clear conception of his own individual worth; he had no understanding of political liberty. He was not a citizen but a subject who marched to the command of a ruler whose power originated with the gods. As such, royal power was not imposed upon an unwilling population, but was religiously accepted and obeyed. . In contrast, the Greeks saw the state as a community of free citizens who made laws in their own interest. To them law was not an expression of whim or divine commands but of reason, not of might but of justice.

Underlying the Greek achievement was a humanist attitude toward life. The Greeks expressed a belief in the worth, significance, and dignity of man; they called for the maximum cultivation of human talent, the full development of human personality, the deliberate pursuit of excellence. By discovering theoretical reason, by defining political liberty, and by affirming the worth and potential of the human personality, the Greeks broke with the past and founded the rational and humanist tradition of Western Civilization.

It is precisely this tradition of secular humanism which the West has esteemed since the Renaissance that Toynbee questioned and challenged. For Toynbee, Greek humanism was an expression of "man-worship," that is, it glorified man and his works; man not God was central to the world-view of Hellenism and this is what caused its downfall. The

great failing of the ancient Greeks, insisted Toynbee, was that they "saw in Man, 'the Lord of Creation' and worshipped him as an idol in place of
God."[2]

Toynbee's interpretation of Hellenism is crucial to his understanding of the nature, meaning,
and destiny of the West. Hellenism provided Toynbee with a structural model by which to examine the
breakdown and disintegration of civilization in
general. It also provided a moral lesson: modern
Western Civilization is a revival of the secular
humanism of the ancient Greeks and suffers from the
same defect -- an overvaluing and worshipping of
man's creations. Toynbee viewed Greek humanism as
"the most whole-hearted and uncompromising practice
of man-worship that is on record up to date."[3] It
was precisely this glorification of man and his
works, said Toynbee, that lead to Hellenism's
breakdown and disintegration, and it is a similar
attitude that is the principal threat to modern
Western Civilization. Because Toynbee derived his
patterns of growth and decline from Hellenic civilization and applied these patterns to the modern
West, we must examine in some detail his structuring of classical history.

Toynbee interpreted classical antiquity in the
light of the theory of challenge-and-response. The
Greek city-state represented a creative response to
the challenge of anarchy that burdened Hellenic society in its formative stage, the Dark Ages that
followed on the ruins of Minoan-Mycenaean civilization. Formed by the union of a number of smaller
communities, the city-state provided its inhabitants with a viable political unity that brought
security during an age of disorder. By engaging in
colonization when threatened by overpopulation and
food shortages, the city-states again responded
successfully to a challenge. In addition to enabling the Greeks to overcome the problems of anarchy
and stringency, the city-states stimulated cultural
creativity. For these reasons, said Toynbee, the
Greeks glorified their city-states, regarding them
as more worthy of devotion than the Olympian gods.
But the city-states did not deserve such devotion,

said Toynbee, for they were not capable of stimulating the individual to his best self. Toynbee saw two defects in the institution of the polis: warfare, which was endemic to Hellenic society, and injustice, for slavery was unchallenged, women had no political rights, and peasants, whose farms were too far removed from the civic centers, found it too difficult to participate in the political life of the city. Despite its considerable achievements, the city-state was still an imperfect human creation, and its undeserved idolization led to the decline of Hellenic civilization.

In the course of the sixth century B.C. the Greek city-states experienced an economic revolution, a change over from subsistence farming to the production of decorated pottery, wine, and olive oil for export that could be exchanged for cereals from Egypt, Sicily, and the Ukraine. This economic revolution, declared Toynbee, necessarily led to greater economic interdependence among the city-states, but this was not accompanied by political interdependence. The new economic circumstances demanded the creation of some form of Panhellenic unity, perhaps a voluntary federation. Could the Greeks meet this new challenge? Could they stop worshipping their city-states and transfer their political allegiance to a Panhellenic body politic? Only such a spiritual revolution could save them from disaster.

The advent of the Persian Wars gave the Greeks an opportunity to achieve the political unity that was made necessary by the accelerating economic unification of the Hellenic world. However, the cooperation displayed by Greek city-states in their victory over Persia did not endure. The half-century following the Persian Wars was a period of cultural flowering, but it also saw the Hellenic world heading toward self-inflicted disaster -- the Peloponnesian War.

Solon had performed a creative act by stimulating manufacturing of pottery and the cultivation of the vine and olives, thereby enabling Athens to overcome the limitations of its poor soil and to become a great commercial center. After the Persian Wars, Athens was in a position to push the Greek world in the direction of unity, but instead Athenian leaders transformed the Delian League into an instrument of Athenian imperialism. The price paid for this decline in the quality of statesmanship was the Peloponnesian War which started the Hellenic world down the path that leads from breakdown to disintegration. This fatal war broke out because Athens had proved unable to conquer the next challenge set by her own outstanding domestic successes -- the challenge of being called upon to create an Hellenic political world order. The Peloponnesian War, said Toynbee, was "the outward visible sign of an inward visible breakdown in the life of Hellenic Society."[4]

By forming the polis Hellenic society had responded creatively to the challenge of anarchy that existed during the Dark Ages; by establishing colonies the polis responded creatively to the challenge of over-population. But the institution of the polis was inadequate to cope with a society growing more complex. Because the Greeks idolized the polis, declared Toynbee, they could not create a Panhellenic political framework to halt fratricidal warfare. The rhythm of challenge-and-response was broken and there was a subsequent loss of self-determination.

The spiritual damage wrought by the Peloponnesian War, brilliantly described by Thucydides, was more significant than the material damage. The atrocities committed both on the international scene and in the civil wars that broke out within a number of city-states were evidence of this spiritual decline. The Peloponnesian War was the price paid for the Hellenic failure to achieve political unity peacefully, a unity required by new economic circumstances. The Time of Troubles was upon the Hellenic world which would be devastated by international and civil warfare with hardly a breathing space for the next four hundred years, until Octavian became master of Rome.

Ninety-three years after the disastrous

Peloponnesian War, the Macedonians imposed political unity upon the Hellenic society for a short period. Toynbee praised Alexander for rising above Greek ethnocentrism to the lofty ideal of a brotherhood of mankind, an ideal to which he himself aspired. However, the premature death of Alexander in 323 B.C. ended the brief period of Hellenic unity and dampened hopes for peace within Hellenic society. After Alexander's death, Hellenic society remained politically fractured, but now into contending kingdoms rather than warring city-states, and Hellenism continued its slide.

In the post-Alexandrian world, the deification of the king replaced the deification of the city-state. But god-kings or priest-kings could not fill the spiritual vacuum that existed in the Hellenic world as a result of the loosening of the bonds between the individual and his city-state.

Meanwhile, the problem of establishing an effective world-polity still remained, but now it was Rome that took up the challenge. By the middle of the second century B.C. Rome stood alone in the Mediterranean world. The Seleucid empire, the Ptolemaic empire, the kingdom of Macedon, and the Carthaginian empire had either been greatly weakened, broken up, or liquidated entirely. By subduing the Hellenistic states, Rome created a universal state that eventually brought order to the Mediterranean world, but she could not reverse the process of breakdown that had begun with the Peloponnesian War. Because the Roman Empire was created by force and much too late, said Toynbee, it could not redeem the afflicted Hellenic society. *Pax Romana* was only a temporary reprieve; coming too late and achieved after years of exhaustive warfare, *Pax Romana* was only a long rally, a peace of exhaustion, uncreative and impermanent, that could not halt the breakdown of Hellenism.

During *Pax Romana* the Hellenic world was no longer convulsed by war and revolution but it was not spiritually rejuvenated. The new cults that prevailed -- deification of the emperor and idolization of the Roman world-state -- were artificial and dull, unable to fill the vacuum left in human hearts that was caused by the decay of the worship of the city-states. The cults of the goddess Rome and the god Caesar, asserted Toynbee, were spiritually bankrupt, and the city-states, no longer centers of bustling political life, had lost their charm and fallen from the ranks of idols.

The Roman world-state, said Toynbee, could not breathe new life into a dying Hellenism. In the process of imposing peace upon the Mediterranean world, Rome had deepened the spiritual vacuum in human souls. While life was more secure, it was also duller, for there existed no ideal that could replace the lost devotion to the polis. The Roman Empire, too vast and impersonal, could not generate the same devotion that had once been extended to the city-state. Nor could the schools of philosophy stir the heart.

CHRISTIANITY

Into this spiritual vacuum, stepped Christianity whose strength, declared Toynbee, lay in its power to restore to Hellenic life some of the significance and enthusiasm that it had lost, and to provide an ideal of human brotherhood that could overcome cultural differences. Christianity offered man communion with a superhuman God of immense stature. Again man had a cause to which he could dedicate himself. The internal proletariat, resentful, alienated, and disinherited, seceded from the old society that was breaking down and gave rise to a higher religion in which gentleness triumphed over violence. A higher religion, said Toynbee, arises within a society that is far along the path of disintegration. It is a response to the challenge posed by disintegration. The internal proletariat seceded from the old order and turned to Christianity, for it treated people with consideration and love; it took care of orphans, widows, the sick, and the aged, and offered an ideal of human fraternity that drew no distinction between Italian, Greek, or Jew, between slave or freeman, between male or female, between rich or poor. As institutions of the disintegrating Roman

Empire atrophied, the Church became the most vital
force in the Hellenic world. The old Roman dominant minority no longer possessed the creativity to
lead and to inspire growth. From the ranks of the
internal proletariat there emerged a new creative
minority to perform in the drama of challenge-and-
response. This new creative minority attracted to
itself the mimesis of the uncreative masses. While
the old society stubbornly fought its losing battle
for survival, a new civilization was germinating in
its womb; Christianity articulated itself into a
universal church which survived the disintegration
and collapse of the old society and carried the em-
bryo of a new civilization.

The internal proletariat was the chief bene-
ficiary of the universal state, for it used the
peace, capital cities, legal codes, common language,
and roads to spread a higher faith. But it was also the external proletariat, barbarians from beyond
the Empire's borders, that benefited from the
world-state, for under the peaceful conditions imposed by the universal state, the dominant minority
lost its zest for combat and the ranks of the army
were filled with barbarian recruits. Eventually
the barbarian external proletariat overran the de-
caying world-state.

Neither Christians nor barbarians destroyed
the Roman Empire, said Toynbee; they merely walked
over a corpse. Hellenism had died before Christianity had become the official religion of the Roman
Empire and before the barbarians had founded their
successor-states on former Roman territory. Hellenism's death was due to its own failure to respond to a challenge that had confronted it in the
fifth century B.C. Hellenic society never recov-
ered from this failure to achieve political unity
through peaceful means. Rejecting Gibbon, Toynbee
maintained that Hellenic civilization had ruined
itself long before the appearance of Christianity.
Churches are not cancers but chrysalides; they do
not destroy civilizations but preserve them by
keeping alive "a precious germ of life through the
perilous interregnum between the dissolution of one
mortal representative of the species and the

genesis of another."[5]

In the interregnum between the collapse of Hellenic society and the emergence of Western society, the barbarians established a number of successor-states. Unlike the Church, said Toynbee, these successor-states were not a creative prelude to Western society but merely an epilogue to Hellenic history. The barbarian states were short-lived, their contribution to Western Civilization insignificant. Both Church and barbarians shared the same stage during the interregnum, but only the Church had an enduring influence on the shaping of Western Civilization. The barbarian achievement was limited to an Heroic Age distinguished by epic poetry; the Church, on the other hand, born of the old society, survived the interregnum to become the soul of the new society -- Western Civilization. Thus the collapse of Hellenism was no disaster for it prepared the way for a spiritual advance; it ministered to the birth of Christianity which for Toynbee is the true soul of the West.

In Toynbee's system, a universal religion emerges after a civilization has entered its decline and it attracts a suffering and embittered internal proletariat. In times of prosperity man remains deaf to the call of the spirit, but during times of stress are found bursts of spiritual activity. The Graeco-Roman world had subdued the orient militarily and offered to orientals a secular way of life in which philosophy would take religion's place. This elevation of the intellect above the heart was not enough either for orientals or for Greeks and Romans themselves. In the form of Christianity the oriental world waged a counter-offensive. Christianity remained at war with the most formidable version of Hellenic man-worship, the worship of the world-state of Rome and its human emperor. "This question whether Man in one or other of his less ungodlike forms is God, or whether the True God is to be found neither in man nor in Non-Human Nature, was, and still is, one of the great issues confronting human souls."[6]

In the late Roman Empire, when classical

values were in decay, Christianity was a dynamic and creative movement. As the institutions of the disintegrating Roman Empire atrophied, the Church became the most vital force in the Graeco-Roman world. After the disintegration of Hellenic society the Church became the source for unity in the emerging Western Civilization. It became the integrating force of the medieval West. The creation of *Respublica Christiana*, declared Toynbee, marked an enormous spiritual advance over Hellenism. Its aim was to replace violence with a reign of spiritual authority and it demonstrated the immense power that religion exercises over human hearts, for devotion to the spiritual church exceeded the loyalty once given to a temporal Roman Empire.

The Christian Middle Ages were very dear to Toynbee. To him the "medieval Western Christian way of life still looks like one of Mankind's rare achievements."[7] The medieval genius lay in shaping a creative balance between papal authority and the secular requirements of princes and city-states, and between theological authority and Aristotelian philosophy and science.

In his earlier volumes, Toynbee regarded churches as links between a dying and an emerging civilization, i.e. Graeco-Roman civilization and medieval civilization. In his later volumes, Toynbee accorded churches a far higher status. Because they embody a higher religion, churches are on a spiritually, higher level than a civilization. Consequently, the breakdown of a civilization is no cataclysm at all if it ministers to the birth of a church, for this is the *raison d'être* of a civilization. A true catastrophe would be the birth of a civilization that emerges from a previously established church.

The emergence of a Christian society in the Middle Ages was a spiritual advance over the Hellenic world, and our current "post-Christian secular civilization might at best be a superfluous repetition of the pre-Christian Graeco-Roman one, and at worst a pernicious back-sliding from the path of spiritual progress."[8] Therefore we should no longer regard our secular civilization as progress, and worthy of our admiration; rather, if we were to think of it

> as one of the vain repetitions of
> the Gentiles -- an almost meaning-
> less repetition of something that
> the Greeks and Romans did before us
> and did supremely well -- then the
> greatest new event in the history
> of mankind will be seen to be a
> very different one. The greatest
> new event will then not be the
> monotonous rise of yet another sec-
> ular civilization out of the bosom
> of the Christian Church in the
> course of these latter centuries;
> it will still be the Crucifixion
> and its spiritual consequences.[9]

THE LIMITATIONS OF SECULAR HUMANISM

Toynbee's conception of the Hellenic and Christian traditions is crucial to his understanding of the nature, meaning, and destiny of Western Civilization. Toynbee, of course, was aware of the immense achievement of the Greeks, but what impressed him more were the limitations of classical civilization. For Toynbee, reason was not man's finest achievement and freedom derived from a non-spiritual source was tenuous. The history of Hellenism teaches what modern Westerners have forgotten or dismissed -- a secular and rational outlook cannot hold society together or restrain man's basest impulses. Unless he is guided by prophetic values, man will deify his state or his leaders, an act that unleashes the worst elements of human nature and causes civilization to break down. The root cause of Hellenism's failure, Toynbee held, was the deification of a human institution -- the city-state and the Roman Empire -- and the deification of a human being -- a Macedonian king and a Roman emperor. By idolizing man in place of God, the Greeks and Romans ruined themselves.

45

Toynbee's dissatisfaction with Greek humanism was at the core of his critique of the modern West which he viewed as a depressing revival of Hellenic secularism and a repudiation of Christiantity, for him the true essence of Western Civilization. Toynbee maintained that since the Renaissance the West has revived the very practice that was at the root cause of Hellenism's ruin -- the deification of the state. Modern nationalism, he insisted, is the modern form of city-state worship; if it is not eradicated the modern world will suffer the same fate as Hellenism.

TOYNBEE AND THE TWO TRADITIONS

Christianity and classical humanism are the principal components of the Western tradition, but they represent two essentially different world-views. The triumph of the Christian outlook signi-fied a break with the essential meaning of classi-cism; it pointed to the end of the world of antiq-uity and the beginning of an age of faith, the Middle Ages. With the victory of Christianity the ultimate goal of life shifted away from achieving excellence in this world through the full and crea-tive development of human talent toward attaining salvation in a heavenly city.

Classicism held that there was no authority higher than human reason; Christianity taught that without God as the starting point knowledge is formless, purposeless, and error-prone. Classicism held that ethical standards were laws of nature discoverable by reason. Reason would instruct in-dividuals about what was best for them; it would enable them to govern desires and will, so that they might order their lives properly; it would show them where their behavior was wrong and teach them how to correct it. Because individuals sought what was best for themselves, they would obey the voice of reason. Christianity, on the other hand, main-tained that ethical standards emanated from the personal will of God. Without obedience to God's will men and women will remain forever sinful; only when they turn to God for forgiveness would they find the inner strength to overcome their sinful

nature. Christianity contended that people cannot
perfect themselves through scientific knowledge; it
is spiritual insight and belief in God that they
require and that must serve as the first principle
of their lives.

It was the Christian outlook that pervaded
Toynbee's philosophy of history. Man by himself
cannot control his own nature or resolve the problems of the community; to be effective reason must
be guided by Christian values. Toynbee considered
philosophy an inadequate substitute for a higher
religion and philosophers lesser figures than
saints. He regarded the moral autonomy and self-
sufficiency sought by Stoics and Epicureans as a
largely selfish aim which forced them to neglect
two emotions -- love and pity -- that are most vital for man's social existence and are the highest
feelings that humans are capable of expressing.
For this reason, Toynbee viewed Stoic and Epicurean
sages as inferior to St. Francis. The whole-hearted feeling of love for a fellow human being can
stem only from religious inspiration and not from
the intellectualism of philosophy. Moreover,
taught by an intellectual elite "in the scientific
language of the Intellect and not in the poetic
language of the Heart,"[10] philosophy cannot stir
ordinary people. By itself the philosophic and
scientific tradition that began in ancient Greece
cannot rescue the modern West, which shows symptoms
of decline. Not the humanist tradition that began
in Greece but Christian spirituality was for Toynbee the most precious ingredient of Western Civilization.

But Toynbee did not reject reason. Like some
of the Church Fathers and medieval scholastics,
Toynbee, the student of Hellenism, was respectful
of the rational tradition. Like Aquinas, who sought
to synthesize Greek philosophy and Christian belief, Toynbee struggled to harmonize the spiritual
values of higher religions with the requirements of
the modern age. But unlike Thomas, Toynbee was a
pluralist who held that all the higher religions
are partial revelations of God's truth.

NOTES

1. W. H. Auden, ed. *The Portable Greek Reader* (New York: Viking, 1952), p. 38.

2. Arnold J. Toynbee, *Hellenism: The History of a Civilization* (New York: Oxford University Press, 1959), p. 10.

3. *Ibid.*

4. *Study*, one-volume edition, p. 171.

5. *Study*, 7b: 392.

6. Arnold J. Toynbee, *An Historian's Approach to Religion* (New York: Oxford University Press, 1956), p. 97.

7. *Ibid.*, p. 169.

8. *Civilization on Trial*, p. 207.

9. *Ibid.*, p. 208.

10. *An Historian's Approach to Religion*, p. 75.

CHAPTER FOUR

TRANSITION TO THE MODERN AGE

The centuries from the Renaissance through the
Enlightenment saw the shattering of the medieval
view of nature, society, and man and the emergence
of the modern mentality. European thought moved a-
way from the medieval division of the universe into
a higher realm of perfection, the source of values,
and a lower realm of corruption inhabited by man.
From Copernicus to Newton there gradually emerged a
universe whose laws the mind could grasp and explain in mathematical equations. To the philosophes
nature was completely autonomous, neither requiring
nor recognizing support or intervention from any
higher source. Like nature, the intellect too was
self-sufficient; it depended upon no transcendent
realm, upon no power beyond itself in order to comprehend the natural world. What the mind did for
nature it could do for society -- through reason a-
lone uncover those general laws that govern the
social world. Through its own powers the mind
could interpret nature and society; it needed no
divine assistance; it accepted no authority above
reason; it insisted upon proof according to standards set by science. The monopoly of intellectual
life by churchmen was ended and science became the
great hope of the future. Rejecting the Christian
concept that evil was intrinsic to human personality
-- a consequence of the defiance of God by Adam and
Eve -- the philosophes held that man was basically
good and that evil resulted from faulty institutions, poor education, and bad leadership.

The shaping of the modern outlook from the
Renaissance through the Enlightenment has been regarded as one of the great episodes in the history
of mankind. But not by Toynbee. He lamented the
decline of Christianity and the upsurge of secularism and regarded the modern West as a vain repetition of Hellenism. For him Christianity was more
than a link between two secular civilizations, a
parent Hellenic civilization and a daughter Western

Civilization. Higher religions are not just by-products of a disintegrating civilization or merely one element among many cultural components of a civilization but new departures. They belong to a distinctive species that is superior to a secular civilization. According to this view there can be no greater catastrophe than the withering of a higher religion.

THE BREAKDOWN OF THE MEDIEVAL WORLD

Toynbee, we have seen, admired the Middle Ages because it held the promise of a Christendom united by spiritual ideals. Such a society, he said, could have dealt creatively with war and politics, two traditions of Western Civilization that did not originate with Christianity but derived from ancient Greece, Rome, and the Germanic warriors. However, to succeed in unifying the West under a Christian banner, the medieval Church would have had to eschew force and remain dedicated to the ideal of God as love. It would have had to demonstrate the spiritual power of a St. Francis, "the greatest soul that has yet appeared in our Western World."[1]

The papacy had acted creatively, stated Toynbee, when it gave unity to a world burdened by feudal anarchy, when it substituted spiritual authority for physical force. But then the papacy soiled its spiritual mission by using force against its opponents; it set "upon a course which was to end in the victory of ... [its] adversaries the World, the Flesh, and the Devil over the City of God which ... [it] was seeking to bring down to Earth."[2] The tragedy began with Hildebrand, who, in seeking to rescue the Church from sexual and financial corruption, was drawn into the arena of power politics in which force was utilized for spiritual ends. This was a dangerous game. Intoxicated by the successful use of force, said Toynbee, the papacy carried it to extremes causing its own spiritual degeneration. The conflict with the Holy Roman Emperor eventually caused the papacy to lose its moral leadership and the devotion hitherto granted to a universal Church was transferred to emerging

50

secular states with disastrous consequences for the future of the West.

> ...this spiritual heritage from the Hildebrandine Church is the element in the constitution of our modern parochial states which has turned these once harmless and useful institutions into a grave menace to the welfare of our civilization. For the spirit of devotion which was a beneficient creative power in Western Christendom when it was directed through the gates of a *Civitas Dei* towards God himself, has degenerated into a maleficent destructive force in the process of being diverted from its original divine object and being offered instead to an idol made by human hands. Parochial states, as our medieval forebears knew, are man-made institutions, useful and even necessary in their place, which deserve from us that conscientious but unenthusiastic performance of a minor social duty which we render, in our time, to our municipalities and county councils. To idolize these pieces of social machinery, which have nothing divine about them, is to court a spiritual disaster; and this is the disaster towards which our modern Western World is heading today as an ultimate consequence of the spiritual spoilation of the Holy See by the secular principalities which were once kept in their place by the Papacy's moral authority.[3]

The establishment of *Respublica Christiana* would have fulfilled the mission of the Church; its miscarriage was "the most tragic of all the disasters that the Western Society has brought upon itself so far."[4]

51

The Renaissance contributed to the undermining of Christendom, for it revived not only Hellenic art and literary forms but also the Greeks' fierce devotion to their city-states. Modern man has remained infatuated with the Greeks and Romans, declared Toynbee, because the ancients taught him how to infuse citizens with patriotic fervor, organize armies, and build a powerful state. This deification of the parochial community was imitated by the citizens of Florence, Milan, Genoa, and the other Italian cities, who allowed loyalty to their local city to predominate over allegiance to *Respublica Christiana*. Machiavelli gave intellectual expression and moral approval to this new outlook. From Machievelli, said Toynbee, was derived the principle that the state was not subject to a transcendent moral law in its dealings with other states. In absorbing and surpassing Hellenic parochialism, the modern West has behaved according to the Machiavellian precept that the state is a non-moral institution. The revival of Hellenism, said Toynbee, ministered to Western man's "insatiable lust for power which was the inevitable ruling passion in hearts that had relapsed from Christianity into a pagan worship of a Collective Humanity," and he pushed "this resucitated political ideology of Hellenism to extremes that had never been approached by the Hellenes themselves in their self-immolation on the altar of an idolized Leviathan."[5] In elevating the state over Christian morality and universalism, the West expressed a defiance of its Christian heritage, conveniently forgetting that this parochialism was the chief cause of Hellenic civilization's downfall. And the same fate will befall the contemporary world, insisted Toynbee, if it fails to "exorcize this demon resolutely."[6]

Another shock to medieval Christendom was the Protestant Reformation which destroyed Europe's religious unity, strengthened the power of secular rulers, and ushered in the brutal Wars of Religion. In these conflicts, religion became a "tool for the furtherance of mundane military and political purposes ... a consequence of Religion's own unprincipaled attempt to use War and Politics as weapons in ecclesiastical struggles for supremacy."[7] Repelled by the violence and fanaticism of the Wars of Religion, seventeenth-century thinkers transferred their intellectual energies from a polemical theology to natural science.

The outbursts of violence and fanaticism during the Wars of Religion, declared Toynbee, alienated many Westerners from their ancestral religion and the new discoveries in science, which seemed incompatible with traditional dogma, intensified this estrangement. The Christian churches that had blundered morally during the Wars of Religion also discredited themselves intellectually by stubbornly retaining a Ptolemaic and Aristotelian science as if this natural philosophy was truly vital to Christian revelation.

The transference of interest away from theology to science was a revolutionary act, said Toynbee. The West would now push religion to the background and concentrate instead on science and technology. In the Middle Ages the inspired saint was the ideal; in the modern age the technician replaced the saint as Western man's ideal and the progressive conquest of physical nature became the overriding concern. As technology moved from triumph to triumph it came to be admired as a magic key that would unlock the door to an earthly paradise. Few recognized that science and technology, unrestrained by religious values, would pose enormous problems for the modern West.

The state system, nationalism, and technology, principal components of modern civilization, have made warfare more brutal than ever. With the breakup of the religious unity of Western Christendom in the sixteenth century, said Toynbee, war became infused with a sectarian religious fanaticism that magnified its evilness. But by the eighteenth century there had been achieved a divorce between war and religion, the immediate effect of which was to reduce the intensity of warfare to the lowest level ever attained in Western history. Warfare in the eighteenth century was relatively civilized -- "temperate and moderate," said Gibbon. Wars were waged for limited aims, casualty rates were low, and the civilian population remained uninvolved. The ferocity and mass emotions that had characterized the Wars of Religion had ended as warfare had been transformed into the "sport of kings," a game played for limited stakes and devoid of passion. Armies were not recruited by conscription and they did not live off the countryside; peace terms were not crushing and countries were not wiped off the map. Princes were forced to wage moderate warfare for there existed no great passion that could rally the nation to a total effort. In the eighteenth century many people regarded war in much the same manner as slavery -- an ancient curse that was rapidly dissipating.

But, said Toynbee, the limited warfare of the eighteenth century turned out to be only a brief interlude between two bouts of fanaticism, the earlier Wars of Religion and the later Wars of Nationality. Once the people had become a "nation in arms" fighting for national survival, warfare could no longer remain temperate and undecisive. During the French Revolution war became an ideological struggle and the flames of hatred fanned by mass emotions could not be extinguished by the rational and universal spirit of the philosophes. The Wars of Nationality, reaching full fury in the twentieth century, would outdo in fanaticism the Wars of Religion.

THE FAILURE OF THE MODERN WEST

In Toynbee's structuring of Western history the emergence of a modern secular civilization out of the womb of *Respublica Christiana* was a "monstrous birth" that marked the beginning of the crisis of the West. A secularized modern Western Civilization, asserted Toynbee, has not transformed human nature with its inherent capacity for wickedness. Indeed, modern technology and administrative procedures have heightened man's criminal potential. The crimes and failures of the modern West compel us to be less complacent and enthusiastic about secularism. Was it a mark of progress that the West articulated itself into warring national states? Did not the break with Christianity take the West down a path that led to total war, genocide, totalitarianism, and nuclear weapons? Did not the rise of totalitarianism show that liberty loses its hold over men's hearts when it is divested of its religious foundation? Has a secularized Western Civilization succeeded in overcoming the two evils that have been the ruin of other civilizations -- warfare and class conflict? Have not profit obsessed Westerners ravished nature and exploited the world's poor? Has Western man's conquest of physical nature enabled him to overcome the spiritual and moral problems of dealing with himself, others, and God?

For Toynbee, Christianity, not Greek humanism or modern liberalism, is the essence of Western Civilization. The West's enduring achievement, he insisted, is not its science but its religion, Christianity, which "will continue to be a living spiritual force for thousands of years after our Western Civilization has passed away."[8] Consequently, the great act of treason committed by Western intellectuals was not the loss of confidence in the values of the Enlightenment, so evident in the twentieth century, but the earlier repudiatinn of the Christian essence of Western Civilization. This effort to "shift the rising edifice of our Western Christian Civilization from a religious to a secular basis ... was the original act of *hybris* which is being requited in our day by an *âtê* that has been accumulating for centuries at compound interest."[9]

NOTES

1. Arnold J. Toynbee, *Christianity Among the Religions of the World* (New York: Charles Scribner's Sons, 1957), p. 73.

2. *Study*, 4: 538.

3. *Ibid.*, p. 543.

4. *An Historian's Approach to Religion*, p. 117.

5. *Study*, 9: 3.

6. *Hellenism*, p. 253.

7. *An Historian's Approach to Religion*, pp. 171-72.

8. *Christianity Among the Religions of the World*, p. 63.

9. *Study*, 5: 411.

PROBLEMS OF THE MODERN WEST:
IDEOLOGIES AND TECHNOLOGY

Consistent with his philosophy of history, Toynbee viewed the problems of the modern West in religious terms. The modern West, he said, has become a post-Christian civilization in which the loyalty once given to Christianity has been transferred to ideologies. The three post-Chrisitan ideologies -- liberalism, communism, nationalism -- are all substitute religions that are in competition with Christian values. Liberalism, said Toynbee, has absorbed the Christian precept of respect for the individual, and communism has adopted the Christian ideal of social justice, but both have broken with the Christian roots of these ideals. A secularized version of social justice and individual liberty is intrinsically inadequate, declared Toynbee. The most pernicious of the ideologies for Toynbee is nationalism, which he regarded as a reversion to the deification of the local community as practiced in the city-states of Sumeria and Greece. Toynbee considered the essential question of our age to be whether the world's higher religions can regain the ground lost to ideologies.

LIBERALISM

The immediate historical roots of liberalism extend back to seventeenth century England, the Enlightenment, and the American and French Revolutions. The struggle for religious toleration by English Protestant dissenters established the principle of freedom of conscience, which is easily transferred into freedom of opinion and expression in all matters. The Glorious Revolution of 1688 set limits on the power of the English monarch and the natural-rights philosophy of John Locke declared that the individual was by nature entitled to freedom and justified revolutions against rulers who deprived citizens of their lives, liberty, or property. From Montesquieu, liberals derived the theory of the separation of powers and checks and balances that sought to guard against autocratic government. The philosophes had supported religious toleration and freedom of thought, expressed confidence in the capacity of the human mind to reform society, maintained that human beings are essentially good, and believed in the future progress of humanity -- all fundamental principles of liberalism.

The American and French revolutions were crucial phases in the history of liberalism. The Declaration of Independence gave expression to Locke's theory of natural rights; the Constitution of the United States incorporated Montesquieu's principles and demonstrated that people could create an effective government; the Bill of Rights protected the person and rights of the individual. In destroying the special privileges of the aristocracy and opening careers to talent, the French National Assembly of 1789 implemented the liberal ideal of equality under the law. It also drew up the Declaration of the Rights of Man and Citizen, which affirmed the dignity and rights of the individual, and a constitution that limited the king's power. Both the American and French revolutions explicitly called for the protection of property rights, another basic consideration of liberals.

In the long view of Western Civilization, liberalism is also an extension and development of the democratic practices and rational outlook that originated in ancient Greece and the value given to the individual by the Judaeo-Christian tradition. Christianity proclaimed the natural equality and inviolable worth of all humans; it insisted that rulers are God's stewards who must exercise their power for the common good; it taught the overriding value of love and charity and it instilled in man a thirst for justice; it held that man was responsible for his actions and must answer for them to God. All this flowed into the liberal-democratic tradition. However, liberals, identifying Christianity with the Old Regime, came to reject the Christian tradition as a barrier to political liberty and social progress. Toynbee called for a reconciliation of Christianity and liberal-democracy.

Toynbee valued the liberal tradition. He favored protection of individual rights, the rule of
law, constitutional government, toleration, and
social justice, and he respected the tradition of
reason. But the liberal tradition, he said, cannot
be a substitute for Christianity and cannot survive
without retaining its link to the spirit of the
Gospels. Divorced from Christianity, liberalism
degenerates into selfish competiveness. Nor can a
self-sufficient liberalism preserve individual liberty or compete successfully with totalitarian
ideologies. To be effective, liberalism must be
infused with spiritual values.

Like nineteenth-century conservatives, Toynbee
held that the liberal stress on self-interest reduces society to a collection of self-seeking and
disconnected individuals whose ighest ideal is
profit. Also like nineteenth-century conservatives, Toynbee rejected the liberal view that evil
is a product of a faulty environment and restated
the Christian view of man's inherent sinfulness.

The tradition of reason, a crucial component
of liberalism, gives man command over nature, said
Toynbee, but this is much less significant than
man's relations with himself, with his fellow men,
and with God. Theoretical reason enables man to
formulate rules that give unity to the phenomenal
world; it does not enable him to enter into communion with the spiritual presence behind the universe or to recognize the Thou of his neighbor.

The liberal conception of personal liberty also suffers from an inherent weakness, insisted
Toynbee. The idea of individual liberty originated
in the Christian belief of the sacredness of the
individual soul. However, liberalism removed the
religious sanction from the ideal of individual
rights. In separating freedom from its Christian
context, liberalism could not fulfill its promised
aim of promoting individual liberty. Conceived
purely in secular terms the liberal ideal of liberty is powerless to contain human wickedness. Nor

could liberalism capture men's souls the way Christianity had; with enlightened self-interest as its leitmotif liberalism was an uninspiring doctrine that could not compete with the totalitarian ideologies. Both communism and fascism offered a spiritually starved Western society an outlet for idealism that had once been channeled into Christianity. To this extent they resembled the theistic religions.

> The common gospel of Communism and Fascism was that, after a spell of unfruitful and ignoble sloth, Man was now at last waking up again to his true nature, which was to live dangerously for mighty ends that transcended the life of the individual. And a convert to this post-war pagan faith might perhaps persuade himself that the stirring times which had sunk into torpor towards the close of the seventeenth century ... were now returning, and that the new 'ideologies' which were the harbingers of this inspiring revolution in human affairs were destined to carry all before them.[1]

If Western liberalism is to maintain itself against the onslaught of totalitarian ideologies, declared Toynbee, freedom must mean more than just secular civil liberty; man must again feel with conviction the original meaning of liberty in the West -- respect for the individual because he has been ennobled by God.

COMMUNISM

An even more formidable ideological derivation from Christianity, said Toynbee, is communism. While Marxists may repudiate religion in general, and Christianity in particular, said Toynbee, their faith could have emerged only in a Christian setting. Marxism began as a Western Christian heresy that attacked a professedly Christian society for not adhering to the ideals of social justice

60

proclaimed by early Christianity.

From Judaism, declared Toynbee, Marxism derived the apocalyptic vision of an inevitable and irresistible revolution decreed by God himself and designed to carry the Chosen People from its low position to an exalted one. Post-Exilic Jews dreamed of establishing through force and with God's approval a great worldly kingdom that would unite all Jews driven into exile. "Marx has taken the Goddess 'Historical Necessity' in place of Yahweh for his omnipotent deity, and the internal proletariat of the modern World in place of Jewry; and his Messianic Kingdom is conceived as a Dictatorship of the Proletariat."[2] Both Post-Exilic Judaism and Marxism conceived their messianic kingdom as a material kingdom of this world; both expected it to be achieved through violence. While the communists have dispensed with the belief in God they have retained the Judaic belief of the Chosen People, viewing the proletariat as the chosen class. Perhaps this predestinarian aspect of communism can be better understood, said Toynbee, by comparing it with Calvinism, another predestinarian sect. Marxism supplied the proletariat of the nineteenth century with the same weapon that Calvinism supplied the bourgeosie of the sixteenth century. The doctrine of historical materialism gave the proletariat confidence that they were favored by the forces of the universe in the same manner that the doctrine of predestination gave assurance to the Calvinist bourgeosie that they were the Elect.

Another Christian element in Marxism, declared Toynbee, is a universalism that has led Marxists, like Christians, to become missionaries of a "Church Militant." "'Go ye into all the world and preach the Gospel to every creature,' is an injunction which Marx feels to be laid upon himself and which he lays in turn upon his followers. ... It is not merely a revolution but a world revolution that the good Marxian is in duty bound to strive for."[3] Having dwelled in a Western society, Marx and Engels acquired the Christian precept, which they never questioned, of converting others so that all might be saved.

In addition to universalism and social justice, said Toynbee, communism has absorbed an unfortunate element of the Judaeo-Christian tradition -- fanaticism. In their conviction of the rightness of their cause, communists "had raised the emotional temperature of a political 'ideology' to a religious heat."[4] In becoming as fanatic as Christian zealots in the Wars of Religion, Bolsheviks displayed some of the worst qualities of human nature and soiled what had been a legitimate struggle for social justice. The Bolsheviks also acquired from Christianity (and from Russian tradition) an authoritarianism that dealt ruthlessly with deviation from orthodoxy. Whereas during the seventeenth century the West had revolted against the passive acceptance of authority, the authoritarian component in the Christian tradition had not eroded in the East, with the result that "a nineteenth-century Russian revolutionary who had rejected the tenets of Eastern Orthodox Christianity might not have shaken off the Christian tradition of authoritarianism."[5]

Communism's appeal, Toynbee believed, has stemmed from its religious nature. It fulfilled a spiritual need created by a declining Christianity; it appealed to man's idealism by giving him a noble cause to which he could dedicate body and soul.

> Man is spiritually frustrated if he
> cannot invest his petty transient
> personal life without abiding spiri-
> tual significance by devoting it to
> some cause that manifestly transcends
> it in spiritual value; and Communism
> proferred to Man an objective that
> might seem worthier than any that had
> been visible on his mental horizon
> since the latter-day eclipse of Chris-
> tianity. Communism called upon post-
> Christian Man to cure himself of a
> childish nostalgia for a justly dis-
> credited otherworldly Utopia by
> transferring his allegiance from a
> non-existent God to a very present
> Human Race to whose service he could

devote all his adult powers by working
for the attainment of an Earthly Paradise.[6]

While both the reformist and universal features of
Marxism are rooted in Christianity, Marxism has
dispensed with a crucial Christian element. Early
Christian socialism, said Toynbee, taught that a
Christian's concern for another's welfare that
leads him to share his worldly goods, "is not a
mere love of Man for Man ... but is a spiritual relation to which God is a party as well as his human
creature."[7] Marx took a Christian principle and
applied it exclusively to the material plane of
life while he denied or ignored Christianity's
spiritual message. Consequently, communism, in contrast to Christianity, cares nothing for the individual human person, his dignity and his need for
spiritual consolation and uplifting. Because it
has dispensed with Christian spiritual values, communism cannot overcome differences between classes,
nations, and races and unify mankind.

NATIONALISM

For Toynbee, liberalism and socialism can be
integrated into the Christian tradition; nationalism cannot. Toynbee defined nationalism as a
"spirit which makes people feel and act and think
about a part of any given society as though it were
the whole of that society."[8] Because nationalism
induces man to deify his community, stated Toynbee,
it is a primitive form of religion. Nationalism
thwarts the vision of the unity of mankind held by
the prophets of all higher religions. Whereas a
higher religion emancipates man from his innate
self-centeredness, nationalism intensifies the brutal and selfish side of human nature. By provoking
fraticidal warfare amongst people that share a common civilization, nationalism hampers social progress. After studying all of man's civilizations
beginning with ancient Sumeria, Toynbee concluded
that nationalism has been responsible for "the
death of no less than fourteen civilizations for
certain, and perhaps of no less than sixteen, out
of the twenty-one civilizations that had come into

existence."[9] Although the spiritual message of
higher religions is infinitely superior to the
nationalist vision, higher religions have not been
able to break nationalism's power or appeal.

In Toynbee's spacious approach to history, nationalism exercises a powerful attraction because
it perpetuates age-old feelings inherited from a
hunting and food-gathering past when men lived in
small separated bands and acquired a tribal sense
of "insiders" and "outsiders." Since the food-
gathering stage constitutes ninety-nine percent of
human history, this tribal attitude toward outsiders became a deeply ingrained habit. The feelings that separated tribes and later villages en-
dured with the creation of man's first civilizations. Impressed with his sensational victory over
nature that enabled him to build cities, man deified his own political community. The gods that
had previously represented the forces of nature now
came to represent also cities and states. The
wind-god Nanna became the god of the city-state
of Ur as later the olive-goddess Athena would become the deity of the city-state of Athens. An
element of religious devotion became injected into
a person's feelings for his city. Thus in ancient
times there already existed a relationship between
nationalism and religion and a potential for fanaticism. Deification of the parochial community,
raised the psychological temperature of city-state
warfare, a pattern that would be reproduced in
other civilizations and with a similar result --
breakdown and disintegration.

Modern nationalism, said Toynbee, sprouted on
soil fertilized by the wreckage of Latin Christendom during the era of the Renaissance and Reformation. The Renaissance's revival of classical culture, one of whose elements was a fierce devotion
to the city-state, raised nationalism to a new
pitch of intensity. The modern West, declared
Toynbee has admired not only the art and literature of Greece and Rome, but also their political
and military accomplishments. The Greeks and
Romans expressed a fierce loyalty to their community, organized effective armies, and engaged in

wars of conquest. In the fashion of the ancient Greek poleis, the citizens of Renaissance Italian city-states glorified the parochial community, thereby undermining loyalty to *Respublica Christiana*.

In addition to Hellenic parochialism, said Toynbee, modern nationalism has been aggravated by Christian fanaticism. While the nationalist has repudiated the Christian concern for mankind and its ideal of love, he has been driven by a fanaticism even worse than that demonstrated by Christians during the Wars of Religion. Convinced that they were in possession of the true faith, religious fanatics during the Wars of Religion sought to impose spiritual unity by force; regarding the nation as the highest good, nationalist fanatics have sought to impose national unity by persecuting minorities and regimenting the population. Nationalism transformed the human community into a god, warfare into a holy crusade, opponents into heretics, and citizens into true believers. That man has been willing to sacrifice himself for this modern cult is an indication that nationalism "was in truth a religious revival in the spiritual vacuum left in human hearts by the evaporation of a higher religion."[10]

Democracy is still another force that has increased the intensity of modern nationalism. At first glance, observed Toynbee, it appears that democracy represents universalism, not parochialism, the rights of man, not the special destiny of a people. But the parochial state has turned democracy into an agent of nationalism, thereby poisoning the political life of the modern world. The democratic state can mobilize all its human and material resources to wage total war. It can use all the instruments of propaganda to arouse the population to a total effort. Democracy has restored to warfare the ferocity of the Wars of Religion. It has transformed the "sport of kings" into *la guerre totale*.

Another force that has contributed to nationalism's "demonic dynamism," stated Toynbee, is industrialism. Like democracy, industrialism is universal in spirit, for it "will not work freely or

65

effectively or beneficently except in so far as the World is organized into one single field of economic activity."[11] But when industrialism made its appearance, the Western world was already broken up into a multitude of petty political-economic units that erected barriers to economic integration. Entangled in the web of parochial states, industrialism, like democracy, has been unable to fulfill its essential nature. Instead of building a world order, industrialism, like democracy, has fortified the parochial state which seeks to promote its own economic interests at the expense of the rest of humanity.

The parochial-minded national state, created in a different social context, was not prepared to cope with the ecumenical forces of democracy and industrialism. The attempt to confine these new and dynamic forces within the framework of the national state, concluded Toynbee, resulted in the totalitarian state. Only a modification of parochial sovereignty could have dealt creatively with industrialism and democracy; perverted by their imprisonment within the national state, these two universal forces contributed to the power of totalitarian nationalism.

The dangerous tendencies in modern Western nationalism culminated in National Socialism which was a repudiation of "the moral and religious essence of ... Western Christian culture."[12] In rejecting Christianity for their human god, Hitler, and his goddess, the German state, declared Toynbee, the German people had adopted a neo-pagan religion. Toynbee believed that Nazism was not a peculiarly German phenomenon but a German expression of the crisis in Western Civilization -- the rejection of Christianity and the return to a primitive religion. The decline of Christianity had created a discomforting spiritual vacuum which was filled by post-Christian ideologies, of which nationalism was the most powerful, and Nazism its most malignant expression. The essential reason why Nazism won over the youth with astonishing ease, Toynbee believed, was not force or propaganda but latent idealism searching for a cause. German youth, no longer nurtured in Christian virtues and morality, embraced the cult of the state, the cult of the leader, the cult of the party, the cult of the race, and the cult of war. The spiritual vacuum that emerged with the decline of religion could not be filled by liberalism, for its stress upon self-interest, utilitarianism, and commercialism could not stir the spirit. To many people National Socialism was a new and inspiring faith.

The experience of National Socialism contains lessons for the West in particular and mankind in general, concluded Toynbee. The Nazi era demonstrated anew the precariousness of civilization and the immutability of human evil. A Germany disillusioned with Western Civilization was retreating into the darkness of the primeval forest where the German tribes had originated. The conversion of the barbarians to civilization had not rooted out barbarism from the Western midst; in the form of National Socialism barbarism "was taking its revenge by finding its way into the souls of its Western conquerors."[13]

Nazism, said Toynbee, was not merely a German response to defeat in World War I. "It marked the consummation ... of a politico-religious movement, the pagan deification and worship of parochial human communities which had been gradually gaining ground for more than four centuries in the Western world at large."[14] That a Western people could fall so low indicates that the West had not risen so high, that it is continually menaced by a perverse barbarism that it harbors within its own breast. For Toynbee, Nazism represented "one phase of the struggle between the spirit of Western Christendom and the spirit of a European barbarism which Christianity had sometimes charmed and had thereby partly tamed, but had never wholly exorcised."[15]

The moral catastrophe of Nazism, insisted Toynbee, demonstrates the inadequacy of liberal humanism. The secular values of the Enlightenment, unbuttressed by Christian spirituality, are insufficient to restrain man's basest impulses. After the Nazi experience it has become impossible to retain a "belief in the inevitable progress of a secularized Western Civilization and in the self-perfectibility of a graceless Human Nature."[16]

While Nazism emerged within Europe among a people that had been Christians for more than a thousand years, it was as much a human problem as it was a purely German or Western one, for within human nature there lurks a vein of wickedness to which Hitlerism makes a strong appeal. The Nazi experience reinforced Toynbee's belief that civilizations are still experiments in which man has sought to rise above the level of the primitive and that these experiments often end in failure.

> The moral is that civilization is nowhere and never secure. It is a thin cake of custom overlying a molten mass of wickedness that is always boiling up for an opportunity to burst out. Civilization cannot ever be taken for granted. Its price is eternal vigilance and ceaseless spiritual efforts.[17]

Toynbee has contributed to our understanding of nationalism. He was correct in regarding nationalism as the dominant spiritual force in modern Western society and he correctly assessed the destructive capacities inherent in modern nationalism. In particular, he called attention to a crucial development in the evolution of modern nationalism. In the process of feeding off democracy, nationalism destroys democracy's essential ideals. Liberalism nurtured nationalism and contributed to its success, but the momentum of nationalism could not be contained by liberal principles.

In the early nineteenth century, liberals identified nationalism with liberty, holding that a unified state free of foreign subjugation was in harmony with the principle of natural rights. They believed that love of nation was commensurate with the universalism and cosmopolitanism of the philosophes. Men must be liberated not only from tyrants and priests but also from foreign oppression.

But as nationalism grew more extreme, it clashed with liberal ideals. In the pursuit of national power, nationalists embraced militarist, imperialist and racial doctrines and lapsed into mythical modes of thought. They rejected the liberal stress on political liberty as an obstacle to national power, supported authoritarian leadership, persecuted ethnic minorities, and denied the ideal of human equality. They elevated loyalty to the nation above all other allegiances and interpreted politics with the logic of emotions. By the beginning of the twentieth century, an intolerant, mythic, belligerent, and racist chauvinism threatened the liberal ideals of reason and freedom. In 1902, the German philosopher Friedrich Paulsen analyzed the danger:

> A supersensitive nationalism has become a very serious danger for all the peoples of Europe; because of it they are in danger of losing the feeling for human values. Nationalism, pushed to an extreme, just like sectarianism, destroys moral and even logical consciousness. Just and unjust, good and bad, true and false, lose their meaning; what men condemn as disgraceful and inhuman when done by others they recommend in the same breath to their own people as something to be done to a foreign country. [18]

By regarding National Socialism as a lower religion, Toynbee has also contributed to our understanding of twentieth-century mass movements. Nazism was in intent a deliberate rejection of the core values of the West. Hitler understood his world-historical role better than did his adversaries:

> To the Christian doctrine of the infinite significance of the individual human soul and of personal responsibility, I oppose with icy clarity the saving doctrine of the nothingness and insignificance of the individual

> human being, and of his continued
> existence in the visible immortal-
> ity of the nation.
> ....
> Providence has ordained that I
> should be the greatest liberator
> of humanity. I am freeing man from
> the restraints of an intelligence
> that has taken charge; from the
> dirty and degrading self-mortifica-
> tion of a chimera called conscience
> and morality and from the demands
> of a freedom and personal independ-
> ence which only a very few could
> bear.[19]

Hitler intuitively grasped the problem of the
West: Western man found the liberal-rational tradition life-denying and political freedom burden-
some. National Socialism was much more than a political movement; it was a new religion, a beguil-
ing mystique, a saving faith. The Nazis shaped a
world-view in which myth was the centerpiece of existence. Hitler glorified the will and intuition
over the intellect and dispensed with objective
truth; Goebbel's cynically manufactured myths that
disarmed the intellect and made the individual vulnerable to manipulation. In typical mythopoeic
fashion the Nazis described the world as a battle-
ground between divine and demonic powers, between
light and darkness. The German super-race, defenders of civilization and goodness, required for its
opposite a demonic race of subhumans with limitless
power for evil and conspiracy. In 1947 SS Captain
Dieter Wisliceny, soon to be executed for war
crimes, astutely analyzed the meaning of Nazi anti-
Semitism. He described it

> as a mystical and religious view
> which sees the world as ruled by good
> and bad powers. According to this
> view the Jews represented the evil
> principle. ... It is absolutely im-
> possible to make any impression on
> this outlook by means of logical or

rational argument, it is a sort of re-
ligiosity, and it impels people to
form themselves into a sect. Under
the influence of this literature millions of people believed these things
-- an event which can only be compared
with similar phenomena in the Middle
Ages such as the witch-mania.

Against this world of evil the race-
mystics set the world of good, of
light, incarnated in blond, blue-eyed
people, who were supposed to be the
source of all capacity for creating
civilization or building a state. Now
these two worlds were alleged to be
locked in a perpetual struggle, and
the war of 1939, which Hitler unleashed,
represented only the final battle between these two powers.

The usual view of Himmler is that
he was an ice-cold, cynical politician.
This view is certainly wrong. In his
whole attitude Himmler was a mystic
who embraced this world-view with religious fanaticism.[20]

Reason employed in the service of myth stripped man
of his dignity and relegated him to the world of
things. It created a laboratory world of soulless
technocrats and dehumanized victims. It forged assembly lines for murder and fashioned an attitude
of mind that killed without conscience.

In his political behavior, twentieth-century
man has demonstrated those illusions, fantasies,
and deep emotional longings that have characterized
the myth-making mentality since the dawn of man.
Myth is a style of apprehending and believing that
reason has never fully subdued. Particularly in
times of stress, men have abandoned rational
thought with its taxing demands for rigorous logic
and objective truth and have reverted to myths
whose simple explanations and simple solutions al-
leviate the anxieties and doubts of tormented souls
and provide the certainty that men crave. In the
twentieth century, myths have taken a new form;

71

political myths are not just the free play of the
imagination, but as Ernst Cassirer points out, "are
artificial things fabricated by very skillful and
cunning artists"[21] in order to bend people to their
will and to rouse the nation to a great effort.
Twentieth-century myths of the class, the race, the
state, the leader, the party, are all expressions
of a perennial irrationality in human behavior, of
an elementary layer of human existence that *logos*
will never obliterate. They remind us that civilized man is never far removed from the attitudes
of primitive man. Concludes Cassirer:

> In politics we are always living on
> volcanic soil. We must be prepared
> for abrupt convulsions and eruptions.
> In all critical moments of man's
> social life, the rational forces that
> resist the rise of old mythical concep-
> tions are no longer sure of themselves.
> In these moments the time for myth has
> come again. For myth has not really
> been vanquished and subjugated. It is
> always there, lurking in the dark and
> waiting for its hour and opportunity.
> This hour comes as soon as the other
> binding forces of man's social life,
> for one reason or another, lose their
> strength and are no longer able to
> combat the demonic mythical powers.[22]

Toynbee understood the dangers inherent in
mythical thinking and recognized the limitations of
reason in confronting these volcanic eruptions of
the irrational.

TECHNOLOGY

For Toynbee, the spiritual vacuum created by
the West's turning away from Christianity was filled
by ideologies, the most dangerous of which was nationalism. Still another idol, technology, attracted a Western soul that had broken with its ancestral religion. Toynbee regarded the rerouting of
the intellect away from a traditional concern with
religion to the domination of physical nature as "a

testimony to the strength and to the repulsiveness of Original Sin;"[23] it was man again behaving as if he were the highest spiritual presence in the universe. And because human nature remains as sinful as ever, man has misused his technological power. In the past three centuries technology has created an artificial environment fraught with danger to the human spirit.

> Man has now decisively overcome Nature by his technology; but the victor has been technology, not Man himself. Man has merely exchanged one master for another, and his new master is more overbearing than his former one. Man is still the slave of his environment; but this is now the environment that he has created for himself, not the environment with which Nature originally endowed him. Nature used to chastize Man with whips; Man's own technology is now chastizing Man with scorpions.[24]

This new man-made environment, said Toynbee, is less appealing than the older one and is a principal cause for world-wide unrest and violence.

Man is finding it increasingly difficult to adjust to the rapid cultural transformation caused by the momentum of technology. The emotions of urban man have been shaped by more than two million years spent as a food gatherer and hunter, said Toynbee, but the intellect has failed to comprehend these emotional needs. The mounting gap between what our intellect conceives and what our heart is capable of absorbing is causing a psychic catastrophe; we are finding it very difficult to adjust to the rapid and revolutionary upheavals resulting from the explosion of science and technology. The cultural change demanded by this ferocious march of technology is causing mankind to reel.

Technology has enabled man to vanquish inanimate nature, but in doing so man has become a slave to his own creations, for the factory hand works at tasks that are inherently impersonal, monotonous, and infantile. The middle class, which in the twentieth century has been abandoning private en- trepreneurship, its traditional field of endeavor, in favor of public service or employment in large corporations, has also felt the pernicious effects of the industrial system. This change from self- employment to working for giant impersonal agencies has altered the mentality of the middle class, for tending "the machinery of a highly organized state administering many millions of subjects was, in- deed, as soul-destroying a task as stoking a fur- nace, minding a power-loom or performing a repeti- tive act of scientifically managed physical move- ments in an assembly plant."[25]

Urban industrial workers and office workers, unlike skilled artisans of the pre-industrial age, take no pride in their work, asserted Toynbee. Having lost their enthusiasm for work, they live only for salaries and for recreation. The psychic strain resulting from the daily monotony of factory and office also leads people to turn to violence for relief. Urban violence is one of the conse- quences of work that is psychologically unfulfill- ing. In engaging in anti-social destructive acts, the bored worker is unconsciously taking his re- venge on society.

The monotony of work is only one cause of the psychological distress that marks our lives in mechanized cities. Pollution, noise, traffic jams, dirt, ugliness, and the separation from nature also contribute to our distress. We earn our liveli- hoods in the cities but seek to escape from them. We live in suburbs, vacation in what remains of the countryside, and spend our retirement in distant regions. We are alienated not only from the work we do but also from the cities in which we labor. In 1969, Toynbee suggested that perhaps we have fashioned a new type of warfare, which may in real- ity be the Third World War, "a war not between states or peoples, but between personality and technology." Underlying student riots, separatist movements, black militancy, and the unrest of the poor, stated Toynbee, "is the effacement of the hu- man personality by the 'brave new world' that has been conjured into existence"[26] by the advance of science and technology. For Toynbee, the Third World War in which we are now presently engaged is a revolt against depersonalization, an expression of rage against a tyrant technology that turns a person into a thing.

The mechanized city of the industrial age has replaced the kind of city that had been familiar to man for 5,000 years, declared Toynbee. Until the outbreak of the Industrial Revolution cities occupied only a small part of earth's surface. Industrialization has altered this pattern. The size and number of cities have increased. Mechanized cities are coagulating into megalopolies which themselves are spreading out and approaching each other. The megalopolies of the world are beginning to coalesce to form a new type of city, an Ecumenopolis -- a world encompassing city broken up only by "surviving remnants of greenery." The new wilderness will not be forests but something more fearful -- "a continuum of streets and buildings." Without intelligent planning the coming Ecumenopolis threatens to become a "world-wide shanty town."[27]

There is also the enormous psychological adjustment confronting uprooted peasants as they stream into the cities. "To be catapulted into megalopolis straight out of Arcadia is to be given a shock that may turn an innocent countryman into an urban criminal lunatic."[28] The new conditions of life and work are intolerable for a former farmer; they distort his human nature.

> Man is not a cipher, not a reference-
> number, not a computer-card; he is a
> living soul. To make his working
> conditions tolerable for him is nec-
> essary, and to achieve this is much,
> but it is still not enough. Man can-
> not live in a state of spiritual
> rootlessness; deracination threatens
> to drive him mad or to goad him into
> taking to criminal courses, and this
> threat hangs over all the hundreds

of millions of human beings who are now streaming into the slums and shanty-towns of the rising World-City out of the villages in which they and their ancestors have been living since the invention of agriculture.[29]

Historically man has felt a close attachment to his city, observed Toynbee, regarding it with love and pride. Thucydides, Saint Paul, Cicero, Machiavelli, Goethe all expressed warm sentiments for their native cities. But inhabitants of modern mechanized cities do not possess these feelings of affection; a general *malaise* prevades our mechanized cities.

The triumphant march of physical science worried Toynbee more than it impressed him, for it was moral and spiritual growth that he considered most important. Moreover, human nature's capacity for evil has been greatly heightened by placing at man's disposal technical facilities of enormous power. While man has expressed enormous pride in his technology, he needs constant reminder that "it is not the essence of humanity, and is not even the feature of human nature that is the most crucial for mankind's existence, survival, and well-being."[30]

Man has demonstrated great skill in comprehending and mastering physical nature, said Toynbee, but he has not shown the same talent for spiritual and moral development. There is an imbalance to man's nature; he has been endowed with much greater ability for comprehending and mastering inanimate nature than for mastering his own nature and for learning how to live in fellowship with others. Since prehistoric times there has existed a morality gap which is "growing wider as technology has been making cumulative progress while morality has been stagnating."[31] Man has not equipped himself spiritually to handle his enormous material power. And in the last three hundred years the gap has widened. Because of our moral backwardness, said Toynbee, we have turned technological advances into social calamities. The most advanced devices of science and technology have been used to commit the worst atrocities in recorded history.

Toynbee consistently warned that we should focus on the limitations of science and technology rather than overrate their achievements. Science has not provided the answers to man's most distressing problems. It has not liberated man from self-centeredness or alleviated his sense of insecurity. The solution to the problems presented by technology, Toynbee argued, is not the continuous acceleration of technology, for growth for its own sake operates like a cancer cell.

In the fifth century B.C., Socrates, finding the theories of the Ionian natural philosophers inadequate for dealing with human problems, turned away from a study of nature to the study of man and society. Toynbee called for a similar reorientation. He yearned for a modern Socrates who would convince man to channel his energies into developing his moral and spiritual potential and would instruct man in the proper use of technology. The techniques and tools created by man's intellect can be enormously effective in bettering the human condition, but "we have not the spiritual power or understanding or goodness to use these tools right. ... We need another Socrates."[32] Perhaps, said Toynbee, in 1956, somewhat prophetically, there will develop in the later decades of the twentieth century "a revulsion against Science and Technology, like the revulsion against Religion in the later decades of the seventeenth century." Former devotees will repudiate what they had adored because they will realize that technology proved "to be a shocking vent for Original Sin and a serious threat to Man's welfare and perhaps even to his existence. If Voltaire were to cast himself for an avatar in the twentieth century, perhaps his warcry, this time, would be: *'La technique, voilà l'ennemi! Écrasez l'infâme!*"[33]

Consistent with his philosophy of history, Tonybee saw a heightening of spiritual energies and a slowing down of the pace of technology as the

answer to the dilemmas of the industrial age. Man
can choose technological regress but this requires
a radical reorientation of his attitudes and prior-
ities.

A heightening of spirituality, declared Toynbee, will turn us away from idolizing wealth and
power which we pursue at the price of personal happiness and social discord. It will lead to a rehumanizing of education, stressing the study of man
for the purpose of improving ourselves and bettering our relations with others. Particularly, if
we learn from Eastern religions, which unlike
Christianity, do not regard nature as something
that God gave man to exploit, we might treat the
natural environment and non-human life with greater
care and respect. Toynbee considered it possible
that a new generation of intellectuals, following
the example of Socrates, will focus on narrowing
the morality gap rather than pushing forward the
frontiers of science and technology.

It should be made clear that Toynbee was not
urging a reversion back to a pre-industrial way of
life. Without modern technology we could never
support the planet's exploding population. What he
wanted was a technological slowdown and a redirecting of our interests and talents toward human needs.
Guided by a renewed spiritual awareness and by new
insights into human nature and human society derived from a transference of intellectual energy
away from technology toward the liberal arts, man
may yet humanize himself and his environment.

In his analysis of the relationship between
technology and civilization, Toynbee reached conclusions consistent with his philosophy of history.
Advances in techniques are not indices of progress;
a civilization may be in decline despite its technological achievements; technology has become for
modern man an object of worship; without the guidance of religious values man cannot learn how to
regulate technology for human ends. We are now
paying the price for this idolization of technology; we have created a monster that can deaden our
souls, destroy our bodies, and ruin our planet.

Nuclear weapons, pollution, and overpopulation, all products of technology, threaten mankind with extinction. By revitalizing our lives with prophetic values, Toynbee claimed, we can acquire the compassion needed to cope with the problems of an industrial age; by redirecting our intellectual energies away from machines toward human needs, we can acquire the knowledge and wisdom to deal effectively with these problems. A technological slowdown, a spiritual revival, and the entrance of our finest intellects into the liberal arts and social sciences offer mankind a hope for surviving the future. In the seventeenth century, according to Toynbee's scheme, man began to explore the universe from a mathematico-physical orientation, breaking with the spiritual world-view of Christianity. Now, three centuries later, we must wrench ourselves away from a singular attachment to mathematics and physics and make a fresh start with a spiritual approach.

We live in a world that is being increasingly united economically and culturally by the exporting of Western science, technology, administrative methods, and education. But the planet remains divided politically because of nationalism, another Western export. The problems posed by technology are not capable of piecemeal solutions, declared Toynbee, but require a world-wide effort. A prerequisite for this global effort is international cooperation on a political level -- some type of world-state.

NOTES

1. Arnold J. Toynbee, *Survey of International Affairs, 1936* (London: Oxford University Press, 1937), p. 23.

2. *Study*, 5: 178-79.

3. *Ibid.*, p. 179.

4. *Study*, 7b : 535.

5. Arnold J. Toynbee, et al., *The Impact of the Russian Revolution 1917-1967* (New York: Oxford University Press, 1962), p. 28.

6. *Study*, 8: 469.

7. *Study*, 5: 585.

8. *Study*, 1: 9.

9. *Study*, 9: 442.

10. *Study*, 7b: 521.

11. *Study*, 4: 169.

12. Arnold J. Toynbee, *Change and Habit* (New York: Oxford University Press, 1960), p. 18.

13. *Study*, 9: 450.

14. *Survey of International Affairs, 1933*, p. 111.

15. *Ibid.*, p. 202.

16. *Study*, 8: 289.

17. Arnold J. Toynbee, *Acquaintances* (New York: Oxford University Press, 1967), p. 294.

18. Cited in Friedrich Meinecke, *The German Catastrophe*, trans. Sidney Fay (Boston: Beacon Press, 1963), pp. 23-24.

19. Hermann Rauschning, *Voice of Destruction* (New York: G.P. Putnam's Sons, 1940), pp. 225, 232.

20. Norman Cohn, *Warrant for Genocide* (New York: Harper Torchbook, 1969), p. 180.

21. Ernst Cassirer, *The Myth of the State* (New Haven: Yale University Press, 1946), p. 282.

22. *Ibid.*, p. 280.

23. *An Historian's Approach to Religion*, p. 288.

24. *Experiences*, p. 326.

25. *Study*, 9: 573.

26. Arnold J. Toynbee, "A Substitute for War," *Long Island Press*, May 3, 1969, p. 13.

27. Arnold J. Toynbee, *Cities on the Move* (New York: Oxford University Press, 1970), p. 34.

28. *Change and Habit*, p. 208.

29. *Cities on the Move*, p. 245.

30. *Change and Habit*, p. 11.

31. Arnold J. Toynbee, *Surviving the Future* (New York: Oxford University Press, 1971), p. 41.

32. *Ibid.*, p. 43.

33. *An Historian's Approach to Religion*, p. 238.

PROSPECTS OF THE WEST

At the beginning of the twentieth century, re-
called Toynbee, Westerners were certain that they
had created an orderly, rational, and satisfying
way of life that would endure. Most Westerners ad-
hered to Gibbon's view that what had befallen Rome
could never happen to the West, for the West had
experienced too much progress in knowledge and industry and the tenacity had been taken out of warfare. Brimming with confidence that they were different from other men, Westerners were certain that
the maladies that had ruined earlier civilizations
would not afflict them and that they would continue
to progress automatically. Toynbee recollected
that before World War I he and his parents

> expected that life throughout the
> World would become more rational,
> more humane, and more democratic,
> and that, slowly, but surely, polit-
> ical democracy would produce greater
> social justice. We had also expected
> that the progress of science and
> technology would make mankind richer,
> and that this increasing wealth would
> gradually spread from a minority to a
> majority. We had expected that all
> this would happen peacefully. In fact,
> we thought that mankind's course was
> set for an earthly paradise, and that
> our approach towards this goal was
> predestined for us by historical ne-
> cessity.[1]

World War I shook the complacency of Westerners and
the crimes of the Nazi era revealed a "criminality
... festering foully below the surface of life in
the Western World."[2] No longer believing in linear
progress, "we have awakened to the truth (how, one
wonders, could we ever have been blind to it?) that
Western man and his works are no more invulnerable

than the now extinct civilizations of the Aztecs and the Incas, the Sumerians and the Hittites."[3]

Does this mean that the West is in decline? To what extent is the West caught in the rhythm of breakdown and disintegration that ruined Hellenism the parent of the West?

THE DECLINE OF THE WEST?

In Toynbee's classification there have been twenty-six representatives of the species civilization. Sixteen of the twenty-six have died. Of the ten living civilizations, three are arrested (Polynesians, Eskimos, Nomads) and in danger either of being annihilated or assimilated by Western Civilization. Of the seven others -- Western Civilization, the main body of Orthodox Christendom in the Near East, the offshoot of Orthodox Christianity in Russia, Islamic society, Hindu society, the main body of Far Eastern society in China, and the offshoot of Far Eastern society in Japan -- "every one apparently, has already broken down and is now in the process of disintegration with the possible exception of our own."[4] But no doubt a Time of Troubles has descended upon the Western world and the West may "have passed its zenith for all that we know."[5]

A society in the process of breakdown falls into "bondage to some idol of its own making."[6] Like the ancient Hellenes, said Toynbee, modern Westerners have worshipped political communities as gods and have engaged in devastating fratricidal warfare. This infatuation with national sovereignty threatens to ruin the West as it had destroyed Hellenic society. If nationalism and world wars are signs of the breakdown of the modern West, what symptoms are there of disintegration?

In one respect the modern West is not confronted with the same situation faced by a disintegrating Hellenic civilization. There are no hordes of barbarians eager to penetrate the borders of a more advanced civilization, for primitive peoples are few and impotent. However, while the West "was conquering the barbarians in the flesh," barbarism, in the form of fascism and National Socialism,

> was taking its revenge by finding
> its way into the souls of its Western
> conquerors. ... and this evil had not
> been exorcized from Western souls by
> the military overthrow of Italian
> Fascism and a German National Social-
> ism; for this perverse Western mani-
> festation of Original Sin was an oc-
> cupational disease of a semi-educated
> urban lower middle class that was as
> ubiquitous as the Western Civilization
> itself, and there was perhaps no prov-
> ince of the Western World in which
> this class was not in some danger of
> succumbing to this malady.[7]

For Toynbee, human nature is the same today as it was for our ancestors, both primitive and civilized. While some superior personalities push civilization forward, even in the most advanced civilizations, the overwhelming majority of people demonstrate a primitive humanity. Thus the barbarism that threatens the West does not take the form of warrior bands beyond the frontiers; rather it manifests itself in a barbarous attitude of mind that has particularly afflicted the lower middle class. Disillusioned with the leadership of the West's dominant minority, the lower middle class embraced a lower religion, fascism. And the attraction of some variant of fascism, said Toynbee, remains an ever present danger in the West.

The ranks of the Western internal proletariat have been swollen, said Toynbee, by recruits drawn from the masses of the non-European world "that had been caught, like the last barbarians, in a world-encompassing Western net;"[8] from uprooted peoples, particularly American blacks; and from the intelligentsia, especially a university educated lower middle class that has no opportunity to use its education. Also included in the ranks of the Western proletariat are ex-farmers forced to move to the cities in search of a livelihood:

> ...the transfer of population from the
> countryside to town has produced the
> same cancer in the Western as in the
> Hellenic body social: the cancer of
> an urban proletariat which has lost
> its roots in the country, has struck
> no roots in the town, and is reminded
> -- every time that it draws its dole
> -- that it is 'in' but not 'of' the
> society which has to serve as the un-
> willing 'host' of this unhappy social
> parasite.[9]

And this is a world-wide phenomenon because Western
Civilization has become global.

Aggravating the tensions between the Western
dominant minority and its global internal proletariat is a color bar. There is irony in the fact
that the Western dominant minority has "been recruited from the Teutonic-speaking descendants of
those White barbarians who had battered on the carcass of a dead Hellenic society some fifteen hundred years back in the past."[10] Uprisings of a
Western proletariat (Jacobins, 1793, Communards,
1871) have been dwarfed by insurrections of a Western proletariat of non-Western origins, so that "a
world-wide proletarian revolt against a world-wide
Western ascendancy had now become a possibility
with which the West had to reckon; and, for a Western Society at bay, this prospect was daunting."[11]
But, concluded Toynbee in 1939, the Western internal proletariat has been spiritually barren, unable
so far to lay "the foundations of a proletarian
universal church or even ... any strong-winged pro-
letarian-born higher religions."[12] In communism,
said Toynbee, a world-wide proletariat has found a
religion that promises it a new Jerusalem but communism cannot regenerate mankind spiritually, for
the Marxist Church Militant uses violence to
achieve its goal and creates a totalitarian state.

In still another way Western Civilization con-
forms to the pattern of disintegration. Hellenic

civilization had experienced two ruinous paroxysms of warfare, the Peloponnesian War and the Second Punic War. The West had its counterparts in the Wars of Religion and the Wars of Nationality, principally the two world wars. The Wars of Religion, symptoms of social breakdown, were followed by a rally made possible by the spread of religious toleration. But the rally proved abortive, said Toynbee, for the principle of toleration, without a spiritual anchor, could not succeed. "The spirits that presided over its conception and birth were Disillusionment, Apprehension, and Cynicism, not Faith, Hope, and Charity; the impulse was negative, not positive; and the soil in which the seeds were sown was arid."[13] That the rally following the Wars of Religion was terminated by the even more destructive Wars of Nationality is the most distressing feature of Western Civilization that enables us to see a pattern of breakdown and disintegration. The "series of two paroxysms punctuated by one rally ... had been the regular rhythm of a Time of Troubles in the histories of civilizations that had run through the whole disintegration process from breakdown to dissolution."[14] However, even if the West is in the midst of a second bout of warfare, what is more significant in terms of its current and potential health is that a universal state has not been created by force, a condition that was avoided by the defeat of Germany in two world wars.

While Toynbee saw signs of breakdown and disintegration in the West, he did not believe the collapse of the West must follow, for man is not at the mercy of an inexorable fate; he does have the capacity to make intelligent choices and to root out those malignancies that have ruined other civilizations. Even though sixteen civilizations have perished and nine others seem in their death throes, Toynbee did not believe that civilizations are doomed inexorably; they are not living organisms predestined to death. Westerners can remedy the evils that afflict their society and breathe new life into their civilization.

There is nothing to prevent our

Western Civilization from following
historical precedent, if it chooses,
by committing social suicide. But we
are not doomed to make history repeat
itself; it is open to us, through our
own efforts, to give history, in our
case, some new and unprecedented turn.
As human beings, we are endowed with
this freedom of choice, and we cannot
shuffle off our repsonsibility upon
the shoulders of God or nature. We
must shoulder it ourselves. It is up
to us.[15]

Rejecting determinism, Toynbee insisted that
the future cannot be predicted on the basis of historical patterns. While maintaining that a pattern
of breakdown and disintegration could be discerned
in the histories of dead and moribund civilizations,
Toynbee did "not believe that this pattern was predetermined or inevitable in any single past case."
Unlike Spengler, he did not postulate "a fixed pattern to which the history of every civilization is
bound to conform." Because "the course of human
affairs is not predetermined" Toynbee was unwilling
"to predict that the Western Civilization will go
the way that a number of its predecessors have
gone." The history of Western Civilization "is today still an unfinished story."[16]

SIGNS OF HEALTH

Although Toynbee saw symptoms of decline in
the West he also recognized signs of health that
make it impossible to predict whether the malady
afflicting the West is lethal. One principal sign
of health is the fact that the West has not yet entered into a universal state created by force. Another sign of health is that while the internal
proletariat might well secede there are "forces of
reconciliation and recuperation that were in the
field against the forces of schism and disintegration."[17] For example, the fact that Venetians and
Lubeckers had been able to transfer their loyalty
from their local city to a larger grouping, the national state, is an indication that Western man,

indeed all mankind, "might one day transfer their allegiance to a universal state between whose provinces war would be impracticable."[18] Toward this end, the movement for European integration is a hopeful sign. Another sign of moral health is the elimination of slavery, an evil that had been responsible for defeating civilizations in the past. Also encouraging for the West has been the compromise between free enterprise and socialism being worked out in a number of countries. Unbridled individualism, said Toynbee, leads only to the domination of the great masses by a masterful minority, whereas "a moderate dose of socialism was a prophylactic against the danger of the society's succumbing to a totalitarianism that would have imposed on human beings the social justice of the antheap and the beehive at the cost of forcibly depriving them of Man's distinctive birthright of freedom."[19] While the spread of education in Western lands is a positive sign, declared Toynbee, it also presents the danger that semi-educated masses would be manipulated by propaganda skillfully prepared by political parties, governments, and businesses; the hope lies in the possibility that an educated populace will acquire the intellectual capacity to detect propaganda. Another reason for encouragement is that Christianity, despite the efforts of Machiavelli, Hobbes, Voltaire, Marx, and Hitler, continues to retain some vitality in Western hearts. "This persistent vitality of a higher religion ... was an element in the Western situation in the twentieth century of the Christian Era that had been conspicuously absent in an otherwise comparable Hellenic situation in the last two centuries B.C."[20] For this reason the West may not succumb to the same fate as Hellenism. An apostate Western Christendom may yet be saved by being born again as *Respublica Christiana.*

SPIRITUAL REBIRTH

If the West is not to go the way of Hellenic Civilization it must return to its Christian roots, for neither our modern ideologies nor science can answer man's need for God or provide a spiritual conception of the individual. Toynbee likened late modern Western man to wanderers in the wilderness, "astray from their forefathers' One True God,"[21] who had succumbed to the temptation of "such devils as Nationalism and Fascism and Communism."[22] In its youth Christianity had fought against the worship of the Roman Empire and the Roman Emperor. Two thousand years later it was engaged in struggle with a modern form of Leviathan-worship, the post-Christian ideologies. That the West has awakened to the dangers of these ideologies is also a reason for optimism. Not only must Western man's spiritual rebirth enable him to overcome ideologies, it must also help him to end his obsession with technology, "his unduly prolonged child's play with clockwork."[23] Toynbee clearly stated his prescription for saving the West.

> In politics, establish a constitutional co-operative system of world government. In economics, find working compromises (varying according to the practical requirements of different places and times) between free enterprise and socialism. In the life of the spirit, put the secular superstructure back on-to religious foundations.[24]

At the heart of Toynbee's remedy for coping with the crisis of a post-Christian West is the need for a spiritual reconversion, but this cannot be satisfied by conventional Christian orthodoxy. "The impulse to indulge in a second bout of traditional religion is, indeed, merely a manifestation on the religious plane of an Archaism, which, on all planes, we have found ... to be a bolt-hole that is always a trap because it invariably proves to be a blind alley."[25] The West cannot reverse history and undo the experience of intellectual enlightenment; it cannot dispense with the rationalism that has characterized late modern Western history. Christianity must not serve as an escape, a hiding place for lost Western souls who would forsake critical thought and make a virtue out of blind authority. Toynbee did not wish to revive the institutional power of churches, but to renew respect for Jesus' precepts of love and compassion.

This would be a true spiritual revolution, whereas a return to traditional orthodoxy would be a dead end. And if Western man "prayed God to grant him a pilot for the perilous passage, he would find the bodhisattva ... whom he was seeking in a Francesco Bernardo of Assisi, who was the most god-like soul that had been born into the Western World so far."[26]

While the kind of progress that men must aspire to is the "cumulative increase in the means of Grace at the disposal of each Soul in this world,"[27] Toynbee recognized that important reforms must be introduced in the secular sphere; without such reforms man might never have this opportunity for spiritual rebirth. However, he insisted that taking the salvation of the individual soul as the supreme aim of life also furthers social progress; there is no antithesis between following God and trying to help one's neighbor.

> In other words, the spiritual progress
> of individual souls in this life will
> in fact bring with it much more social
> progress than could be attained in any
> other way. It is a paradoxical but
> profoundly true and important principle
> of life that the most likely way to
> reach a goal is to be aiming not at
> that goal itself but at some more am-
> bitious goal beyond it. ... Therefore,
> the replacement of the mundane civili-
> zations by the world-wide and enduring
> reign of the Church Militant on Earth
> would certainly produce what today
> would seem a miraculous improvement in
> those mundane social conditions which
> the civilizations have been seeking to
> improve during the last six thousand
> years.[28]

All the higher religions teach us that our wants exceed our needs, that excessive self-indulgence is an obstacle to the pursuit of spiritual aims, and that man has a moral duty to consider his neighbor's needs -- attitudes which promote social progress.

In two ways Toynbee saw Western Civilization as unique. Firstly, of the seven extant civilizations only the West does "not show indisputable signs of being already in disintegration."[29] Secondly, Western Civilization has spread throughout the globe. Thus the destiny of the West has become tied to an emerging world civilization, the product of the outpouring of European ideas, institutions, and technology that began in the late fifteenth century. By adopting Western techniques and the Western state system, the non-Western world has become drawn into Western Civilization's spiritual crisis. But from this world-wide spiritual crisis, hoped Toynbee, there will emerge a universal state imbued with prophetic ideals. This is of critical importance in Toynbee's philosophy of history. From the beginning of human history mankind has been fragmented into different bands, tribes, states, civilizations. And now the West, without intending it, has become an agent of global unity, making it possible to realize the universalist visions of the prophets.

NOTES

1. *Surviving the Future*, pp. 106-07.

2. *Study*, 9: 433.

3. *Civilization on Trial*, p. 37.

4. *Study*, 4: 3.

5. *Ibid.*, p. 122.

6. *Study*, 9: 441.

7. *Study*, 9: 450-51.

8. *Ibid.*, p. 451.

9. *Study*, 5: 164-65.

10. *Study*, 9: 453.

11. *Ibid.*, p. 455.

12. *Study*, 5: 188.

13. *Study*, 6: 317.

14. *Study*, 9: 464.

15. *Civilization on Trial*, p. 45.

16. *Study*, 12: 519.

17. *Study*, 9: 461.

18. *Ibid.*, p. 446.

19. *Ibid.*, p. 448.

20. *Ibid.*, p. 461.

21. *Ibid.*, p. 450.

22. *Ibid.*, p. 449.

23. *Ibid.*, p. 629.

24. *Civilization on Trial*, p. 45.

25. *Study*, 9: 630-31.

26. *Ibid.*, p. 644.

27. *Civilization on Trial*, p. 229.

28. *Ibid.*, p. 216.

29. *Study*, 9: 411.

CHAPTER SEVEN

THE WORLD-STATE

All the strands of Toynbee's philosophy of history coalesced in his concept of the coming world-state. In this utopian vision he demonstrated again his hatred of nationalism, his fear of technology, and his concern for the individual.

The crisis of the West, said Toynbee, has now become part of a world-wide crisis; it is no longer a question of the West declining but of mankind perishing. For a humanity threatened with extinction by the lower religion of nationalism and the power generated by an idolized technology, Toynbee prescribed a universal state and a revitalization of spiritual ideals.

Because of war, maintained Toynbee, civilizations can only be regarded as experiments in which man has sought to rise above the level of the primitive. Just when it seems that man has pulled ahead, he again defeats himself by succumbing to war. And what has exacerbated warfare and wrecked civilizations more than anything else has been the absolute sovereignty and unqualified loyalty demanded by states; it is imperative that mankind break with the system of parochial states.

Toynbee believed that a political system's merit depends on its ability "to rid human social life of the violence that is the price of anarchy."[1] Judged by this standard, world-states have been considerably more successful than city-states or national states; they have succeeded in providing a large measure of domestic order and unity while engaging in relatively few wars with states beyond their borders as was the case of Rome in the two centuries after 27 B.C. To build a world-state is the great challenge facing mankind today, insisted Toynbee.

Toynbee maintained that humanity possesses the administrative and technological means to solve the problems of our industrial age, but there is a political barrier to effective action. Although the whole of mankind is being knit together economically and culturally by the outpouring of Western parliamentary government and industrialism, it remains divided politically and ideologically. But only a world government can deal effectively with the interrelated problems of the global age -- nuclear weapons, pollution, overpopulation; the survival of mankind depends on man's ability to create a global federation. But if it is to succeed and endure such a world-polity must rest upon a spiritual foundation, for purely human bonds cannot hold mankind together: "The only society that is capable of embracing the whole of Mankind is a superhuman *Civitas Dei*; and the conception of a society that embraces all Mankind and yet nothing but Mankind is an academic chimera."[2]

While political divisiveness is as old as the first hunting bands, declared Toynbee, world-mindedness is a relatively recent phenomenon making its appearance only after civilization had already established itself. A world-state was formed when one state delivered a knock-out blow to its competitors, but the age-old habit of divisiveness inherited from the early days of prehistory continued to persist. Conquered peoples often rejected the peace and stability imposed by the world-state and rose in nationalist revolt. In our own day, the subordination of the universal elements of communism to the demands of Russian nationalism demonstrates anew the greater attraction of parochial-mindedness. Yet world-states have not been without their appeal as evidenced by the loyalty Rome received from the different peoples that comprised the Empire. Historically world-states were established through conflict and conquest, but at a prohibitively high cost. While these world-states succeeded in imposing universal peace upon a war-stricken society, they could not cure the spiritual disorders caused by centuries of war; they could only temporarily arrest, but not reverse the society's downhill slide. For Toynbee, the solution for the problems posed by national sovereignty is the creation of a world-state by *consent*, not by force, before the process of breakdown and disintegration is well advanced. Modern weapons rule out the traditional way of creating a world-state, for atomic warfare would only unite mankind in death. Despite the persistence of nationalism, and even its growing intensity in some parts of the world, Toynbee believed that the creation of a global polity is not beyond man's capacity. A number of unifying tendencies exist today powerful enough to overcome formidable historical and psycholgical barriers to a world-wide state.

While tribalism is a deeply ingrained and formidable habit, said Toynbee, it is still a product of culture and not an ineradicable trait of human nature. Toynbee felt that man can be taught to regard a world-state as a superior form of political organization and he can learn to subordinate local loyalty to a world-wide loyalty. Since 1500 certain developments have served to push mankind together into the direction of a single society. The agent in this movement toward globalism has been the West. This is ironic, for while Western Civilization achieved cultural unity, it has been notoriously plagued with political parochialism.

Since 1500 the West has been spreading its technology, institutions, and ideas throughout the globe, bringing together the once separate societies into a common culture. This cultural unity, spurred by the annihilation of distance resulting from modern transportation and communication, might serve as the prelude to political unification. Spearheading the diffusion of Western civilization and the rise of world cultural unity is a world-wide intelligentsia comparable to the Hellenizers who served as the medium for the cultural unification of the ancient Mediterranean world. Perhaps the modern intelligentsia, many of whom already think and behave as world citizens and share a common Western Civilization, will provide the social and cultural bonds to hold together the world-state. The intelligentsia is producing Western style nation states throughout the globe that "are going to be uniform enough to serve as cells for the construction of a world-wide world-state, as the city-states standardized on the Hellenic pattern once served as cells for the construction of the Roman world-state."[3]

Another promising sign for future world unity, said Toynbee, is the growing economic and political consolidation of Western Europe since World War II and the discrediting of romantic nationalism. This radically new departure "is a good augury, considering how deeply ingrained is nationalism in the tradition of Western European peoples and how often one or another of them has tried to subjugate the rest by force. If the Western European peoples can unite with each other voluntarily, as they are now demonstrating they can, a voluntary unity of mankind, on a global scale is not a utopian objective."[4] Since World War II Western Europe has also displayed a distaste for militarism, a psychological revolution that reversed a tide that had been flowing since the opening of the modern era, except for one pause in the eighteenth century.

A world society requires that people share ideals and manners. Can mankind attain a stable political unity without at the same time achieving ideological and religious unity? Does a world political federation require uniformity of ethical standards and ideals? Toynbee did not believe that ideological and religious variety are incompatible with political unity so long as there is no accompanying animosity and competition for power. Is this possible? The answer to this question is related to the larger matter of Toynbee's vision of the coming world-state.

The future world-state will not be greatly centralized, said Toynbee, for the peoples of the world will only support world government reluctantly. Moreover, in an era of atomic weapons recalcitrant national states cannot be coerced into accepting world authority. States will not put themselves out of business, but will surrender some prerogatives for the sake of self-preservation. Realizing that the alternative may be self-destruction, declared Toynbee, mankind will choose a form of world government, but unlike the world-states of the past, which were unitary states imposed by force, the coming world-state will be a voluntary federal union. However, it must have the power to prevent local units, driven by parochial loyalties, from engaging in war. It is possible that over the years the loyalty that had once been directed to the national state may be transferred to mankind as a whole.

Toynbee feared that the coming world-state will be a dictatorship, for periods of social anarchy are often followed by autocratic rule as was the case of the Roman Republic in the first century B.C. In 1971, Toynbee speculated that by the year two thousand the world would be held together "by a atrociously tyrannical dictatorship," controlled perhaps by cliques of military men from different regions. This future dictatorship might "be imposed on the majority by a ruthless, efficient, and fanatical minority, inspired by some ideology or religion."[5]

While the lessons of history seem to indicate that the coming state will be a dictatorship imposed by a minority, Toynbee still held out hope that it would be created by voluntary agreement and would allow for participation in government which "is one of the natural human rights of every individual." But because self-annihilation looms if we fail to unite, "we cannot afford to wait till we can be sure of being able to build democracy into the world-state's original constitution."[6]

Ideally, Toynbee envisioned an eventual world government with sufficient power to abolish wars. National states would exist as federated units. To humanize Ecumenopolis, said Toynbee, it will have to be broken up into numerous small, self-contained, sub-units, the size of an ancient Greek city-state or a medieval town. Each of these sub-units would be adjacent to a country area that would remain permanently undeveloped. Within these cities there would be still smaller units, wards that would promote a sense of neighborliness. They would be so designed that youngsters could go to school and housewives shop without having to cross streets travelled by autos. The intimacy of the rural village will be transplanted to urban areas and men will have a chance of feeling once more members of a community. By decentralizing the world-city we can cure the loneliness of city life and ease the transition for the multitudes of new city dwellers arriving from the countryside. By restoring a sense of community to inhabitants of cities, by treating them as persons and not as things, serial numbers or ciphers, and by heeding their legitimate grievances, we can reduce the level of violence.

Besides his affiliation to a local ward in the coming world-city and his loyalty to the future world-state in which he holds citizenship, there is still another community to which the individual could belong and from which he could derive gratification -- a world-wide diaspora of people sharing common professional interests. Russian physicists, for example, have more in common with American scientists than they do with Russian farmers. Similarly, the world's doctors, mathematicians, musicians, artists all form a community of their own that crosses state frontiers. These people, meeting in international societies and communicating by letter, telephone, and on television screens, will serve as another bond of world unity.

To facilitate an attitude of world-mindedness, schools will have to require fluency in at least one foreign language and attempt to reduce race consciousness. While race feeling is an obstacle to the unity of mankind, there are many examples of peoples -- Hawaiians, Mexicans -- who are relatively oblivious to racial differences. Toynbee believed that the bonds of common culture and common religion are strong enough to overcome racial differences.

100

On the basis of historical experience, Toynbee did not want the future world-state to suppress completely local variety and autonomy for a standardized global culture and a centralized universal government. Such conditions tend to produce cultural deterioration and social stratification. "The Roman Empire prospered under the principate, when it was administered as a commonwealth of still autonomous, but no longer sovereign, city-states; it decayed with the decay of local autonomy and with the transformation of the world-government from an instrument for keeping the peace into an agency for the centralized bureaucratic administration of local as well as common affairs."[7] It will be the task of good statesmanship to create a harmony between the national and the universal. But if this is to endure and succeed, "the authority of the 'universal', and the loyalty paid to it, must be paramount."[8]

Toynbee hoped that religious or ideological variety will not be obliterated by future political unity. Through education, children will learn about all the world's ideologies and religions, and, hopefully, differences will become a stimulus for choice rather than a cause for irrational hate. Moreover, the problems confronting mankind -- "urbanism, pollution, psychological disorientation, and outbreaks of irrational violence ... transcend the traditional differences between ideologies."[9] And as both capitalism and communism become more flexible and pragmatic, ideological issues will seem less important.

SPIRITUALITY AND SOCIAL JUSTICE

Consistent with his interpretation of history, Toynbee believed that the coming world-polity needs a religious base. Only by embracing prophetic values can man overcome the limitations of parochialism and live in brotherly unity. Western technology is an inadequate scaffolding upon which to construct a world-state. Only by turning to the religious prophets of universalism -- Isaiah, Jesus, Buddha, Gandhi -- can man shape an enduring world order, for "there can be no unity of Mankind without the participation of God."[10] The leap from tribalism to ecumenicalism requires a religious revolution, but Toynbee recognized that man is still far from this stage.

According to Toynbee's world-view, fratricidal wars between states and conflicts between classes caused by injustice have been the principal reasons for the ruin of civilizations. The future world-state must not only be powerful enough to save humanity from committing suicide through nuclear warfare, it must also promote human welfare through a radical redistribution of the planet's goods. For the past five thousand years, stated Toynbee, the masters of the civilizations have terribly exploited the lower classes. The achievements of civilization have been built on the backs of peasants, but these unfortunates have continued to live at a starvation level. The favored few have defended their selfishness by insisting that they were trustees for all future generations. In a world of scarcity, the fruits of civilization had to go to a few or there would be no fruits at all and humanity would be deprived of its future. While this plea might have had some validity in the past, said Toynbee, our unprecedented progress in technology makes it invalid today. Yet some 3/4 of humanity currently live below the poverty line struggling for survival as did our early ancestors. In the past the exploited masses had docilely accepted poverty, but in the twentieth century this habit of resignation has been broken. For Toynbee, the world revolution of the peasantry for social justice is not only the dominant theme of the age, it is also "the most glorious *secular* revolution"[11] in world history. Throughout the world the poor are abandoning their fatalism and are demanding freedom from want; the cry for economic equality can no longer be silenced. This emancipation of the world's poor and oppressed, Toynbee was certain, will "stand out in retrospect as the epoch-making event of our age."[12] It is the West that deserves credit for this hopeful development "for it has not only conceived the ideal of social justice; it has also conjured up the material means for translating this ideal into practice."[13]

Toynbee found in the Judaeo-Christian tradition the source of the Western concept of social justice that is now becoming world-wide. Christianity has preached the dignity of every human being regardless of wealth or status; it has proclaimed that all men are entitled to spiritual justice. In the eighteenth century "the demand in Western Christendom for social justice overflowed from the religious into the secular province of social life."[14] The philosophy of the Enlightenment and the anti-slavery movement were secular applications of the Christian principle of social justice. But this secular demand for social reform would have been only utopian had not the Industrial Revolution simultaneously given man the tools by which he could realize the ideals of social justice. There has been a tragic facet to the movement for social justice, declared Toynbee. While it began within the bosom of religion and then overflowed into the secular arena, the established churches did not take an active part in this new orientation, but "stayed within their customary ecclesiastical bounds and left the cause of secular social justice to be championed by laymen who were indifferent to religion if not positively hostile for what seemed to them a callous betrayal of its mission."[15] If religion is to regain its former influence, concluded Toynbee, it will have to campaign more vigorously for social justice. For Toynbee, a religious society will be more successful than a secular one in achieving social reform. The spiritual progress that higher religions seek by having man draw closer to God will also result in an improvement in human material welfare.

How is the ideal of social justice to be realized in the future world-state? Certainly not by any dogmatic allegiance to either capitalism or communism. Toynbee rejected the doctrine that private profit is a sacred human right: "untrammeled freedom for economic private enterprise means freedom in this line for the small minority that commands the economic means for taking advantage of freedom here."[16] But for the great mass of ordinary people it does not mean freedom at all. Toynbee maintained that a mixed system of private enterprise and socialism offers the best solution. The proportion of the blend would be determined not *a priori* but according to experience and would be subject to modification.

On a political level, Toynbee sought a golden mean between the unrestricted sovereignty of national states and the unrestricted authority of a centralized world-state. On an economic level, he favored a mean between unrestricted private enterprise and unmitigated socialism. The American ideology, he said, stresses individual freedom but is not sufficiently concerned with social justice; on the other hand, the Russian ideology stresses social justice and dispenses with individual freedom. The middle way, which Toynbee saw developing in Western Europe, might prove to be the model for the non-Western world. Wise statesmanship, said Toynbee, should not attach itself to an ideology, capitalist or communist, that is regarded as a semireligious faith; it should not turn to ideologies as panaceas for society's ills. Rather, it should strive for practical common-sense solutions to particular problems.

Toynbee valued individual liberty but felt that left uncurbed it leads to oligarchy, for it gives "a free hand to a minority who, in an unrestricted competition of all against all, are more than a match for the rest of the community in physical strength, mental ability, wealth, or political power."[17] By giving full scope to personal liberty, social justice is violated. But to pursue social justice with single-minded devotion is to suppress personal liberty which "is an indispensible condition for any human achievement."[18] In his hostility to fanaticism, in his opposition to doctrinaire thinking, in his stress upon balance and moderation, Toynbee displayed some of the qualities of British pragmatism.

Toynbee believed that the gap between rich and poor could be narrowed by a world-state sufficiently strong to tax the richer nations for the benefit of the poorer ones. As an immediate step, he urged the poor nations to form an international union

that would emulate the militancy of labor unions:
"If the poor majority of the World's countries were
to strike collectively, by refusing to sell to the
rich countries their labor, their raw materials,
and their foodstuffs, except on more equitable
terms, I believe that they could compel the richer
countries to change the terms of trade to the poorer countries' advantage; and this would be a victory for justice."[19] Both developments -- the taxing of the rich and the growth of the power of labor unions -- had in Toynbee's life time helped to
close the gap between the classes in England. He
believed they now needed a world-wide application.

Toynbee's other proposals to promote social
reform in the future world-state included government sponsored birth control, expanded education,
and the redirecting of funds away from armaments
and space exploration toward feeding and clothing
the wretched of the planet. Toynbee regarded the
space program as a great adventure, but likened it
to the pyramids and the palace of Versailles --
masterpieces of human skill and cooperation built
at the expense of the poor majority and therefore
morally offensive. We should also stop manufacturing products that satisfy bogus wants conjured up
by Madison Avenue and direct our productive capacities toward fighting a world-wide battle against
poverty. To survive the future, said Toynbee, we
shall have to alter the notion that the fruits of
technology belong only to the immediate producers;
instead we shall have to share with the whole of
mankind the material wealth produced by technology.

The world-city must not only meet man's material needs, but it must also provide him with an
outlet for his spiritual energies. Technology
should assist man in achieving the true purpose of
life, which is spiritual. Toward this end, we
shall have to reeducate industrial man, enabling him
to make proper use of his leisure so that he finds
satisfaction in "thought and art, and religion ...
the fields in which the spiritual side of human nature can find infinite scope. ... If we can succeed
in doing this, we may see a new flowering of culture -- a second Renaissance -- instead of the

development of a parasitic society, which, like the urban proletariat in the Roman Empire, lives for 'bread and circuses' and turns savage if it is not given to them."[20]

A heightening of spirituality will turn us away from idolizing wealth and power which we purchase "at the price of individual unhappiness for ourselves and of discord with each other."[21] It will lead to a rehumanizing of education stressing the study of man for the purpose of improving ourselves and bettering our relations with others. Toynbee considered it possible that a new generation of intellectuals, following the example of Socrates, will focus on narrowing the morality gap rather than pushing forward the frontiers of science and technology. He saw signs of such a reorientation occurring in the United States in the last third of the twentieth century. Guided by a renewed spiritual awareness and by new insights into human nature and society obtained by the transference of intellectual energy away from technology to the liberal arts, man may yet use technology and science to humanize the coming world-city. Particularly if we learn from Eastern religions, which unlike Christianity, do not regard nature as something that God gave man to exploit, we might treat the natural environment and non-human life with greater care and respect.

Toynbee warned that the struggle for social justice should not be accompanied by educational egalitarianism which stifles gifted children and reduces schooling to the lowest common denominator. The doctrinaire egalitarians damage the public interest, for exceptional individuals have always been civilization's pacesetters. Hopefully, the individual with unusual ability will recognize his "moral obligation to use his gifts, not in Napoleon's way, just for his own selfish advantage at his less gifted fellow men's expense, but, if he can rise to this height, in a bodhisattva's way -- that is to say, at his own expense for the benefit of all other sentient beings."[22] In this way he achieves self-transcendence.

Ultimately the solution to human problems requires a religious orientation, insisted Toynbee. That these problems could only be solved "by lifting them from the social to the religious plane was as true in a twentieth-century Westernizing world as it had been true always and everywhere since the transfiguration of Sub-man into Man."[23] God, as Saint Paul proclaimed, had "made of one blood all nations of men," and in the same spirit Saint James taught "that he who loveth God loves his brother also." It is in this spirit that man must approach the problem of social justice.

For Toynbee, the true end of human life can never be the accumulation of enormous amounts of consumer goods as dictated by advertising industry. What distinguishes man from non-human creatures with whom he shares the planet is that only he has a spiritual purpose in life. In pursuit of this spiritual end, said Toynbee, man needs only a small quantity of consumer goods. Man's wants have always exceeded his real needs even before advertising inflated them. Higher religions have consistently cautioned us "against excessive self-indulgence in the satisfaction of our material wants because they hold, and rightly hold, that this is an obstacle to attaining the true end of Man -- the true end of Man being the pursuit of spiritual aims."[24] All the higher religions have exhorted man to recognize his moral responsibility to his fellow man and to care not only for his own needs but also for those of his neighbor. In today's world, said Toynbee, this commandment is directed especially toward the rich Western minority. Toynbee urged Westerners to abide by the religious virtue of self-denial in order to care for the suffering poor throughout the globe. If Americans could take the lead the rest of the Western world would follow, guided "by the voice of religions."[25]

Future generations, said Toynbee, may look back upon the present materialism of the West with feelings of astonishment and even disgust and shame that so much energy was squandered trying to obtain immoderate amounts of material possessions. They will have arrived at a much healthier estimation of the amount of goods a man really needs in order to allow for spiritual development. Western man, who has sacrificed his soul by an over enthusiastic concentration upon material goods, can redeem himself by utilizing his technology for the good of all humanity.

If the future world-state manages to rid itself of war and class conflict that have traditionally wrecked civilizations and succeeds in coping with pollution and over-population, the next problem confronting mankind would be the role of leisure in a mechanized world. In the past only a minority had the self-discipline and self-education to utilize leisure creatively. This creative minority had given to mankind a priceless cultural treasure. The attitudes and interests of this creative minority are not easily transmitted. Toynbee feared that the lavishing of leisure on the unprepared masses would lead to cultural deterioration. What irony it would be if the reward for the elimination of war and class conflict turns out to be the wallowing for ages in a "commonwealth of swine." To prevent the coming world-state from becoming Huxley's "brave new world" or Plato's "commonwealth of swine," leisure must be utilized creatively. Technology is creating an abundance of leisure, but industrialized man "often positively dreads leisure because it confronts him with his own self, isolated terrifyingly in the 'lonely crowd.'"[26] Modern man spends his leisure in a "sub-human" way, principally as a passive spectator of television and sporting events. The society of the future must provide an educational system that stimulates aesthetic and intellectual growth. But while only a relatively few people possess the intrinsic gifts required for art or thought, religion provides "an infinite spiritual scope to Everyman."[27] It is the finest outlet for leisure.

Was Toynbee optimistic about the future? While granting that in the twentieth century material wealth has increased and in many instances conditions for the poor have improved, he noted that there has occurred, what nobody foresaw in 1914, a "great moral regression in people's treatment of each other." In the year 1971 the Western world was "much less humane than it was in 1913. We have to face the possibility that the World will become still more inhumane by the end of the present century."[28] Our Westernizing world in the twentieth century, said Toynbee, reveals extraordinary contradictions. At the same time that humanitarian feelings, as expressed in a concern for the human rights of all people, have risen to new heights, the cruelties of class warfare, nationalism, and racialism have shown man at his worst.

However, despite the difficulties burdening the world, Toynbee remained hopeful. We have the intellectual ability to cope with war, overpopulation and pollution, but the head must persuade the heart to renounce cherished and longstanding practices. Human beings have the capacity to choose life over death, good over evil, said Toynbee, and in the methods of Gandhi and Martin Luther King we have the proper guide. Toynbee felt that man, however reluctantly, tardily, or sulkily, will choose life over suicide by renouncing the institutions of sovereignty and war, so dear to human hearts. If humanity forsakes tribal-mindedness and false gods and becomes imbued with universalism and spirituality, from its sufferings it will have acquired wisdom.

NOTES

1. *Change and Habit*, p. 24.

2. *Study*, 6: 10.

3. *Change and Habit*, p. 155.

4. Arnold J. Toynbee, "For the First Time in 30,000 Years," *Worldview* 15 (March 1972), 9.

5. *Surviving the Future*, p. 113.

6. Arnold J. Toynbee, *America and the World Revolution* (New York: Oxford University Press, 1962), p. 67.

7. *Study*, 12: 618.

8. *Ibid.*, p. 619.

9. *Surviving the Future*, p. 142.

10. *Study*, 7b: 511.

11. *America and the World Revolution*, p. 86.

12. *Ibid.*, p. 40.

13. *Ibid.*, p. 41.

14. *Ibid.*, p. 161.

15. *Ibid.*, p. 199.

16. Arnold J. Toynbee, *Between Niger and Nile* (New York: Oxford University Press, 1965), p. 84.

17. *Study*, 9: 593.

18. *Ibid.*

19. *Surviving the Future*, pp. 134-35.

20. Arnold J. Toynbee, "Mankind's Moral Malady," in Larry Ng, ed. *Alternatives to Violence* (New York: Time-Life Books, 1968), p. 159.

21. *Surviving the Future*, p. 43.

22. *Experiences*, p. 347.

23. *Study*, 9: 594.

23. *America and the World Revolution*, p. 145.

25. *Ibid.*, p. 149.

26. *Surviving the Future*, p. 93.

27. *Ibid.*, p. 618.

28. *Surviving the Future*, p. 107.

ASSESSMENT

In many ways the thought of Arnold Toynbee
seems strangely out of place in the twentieth century. While scholars in the various disciplines
have been carving out still narrower areas of specialization, Toynbee chose to write a universal
history. In an age of intellectual fragmentation,
he suggested a comprehensive meaning behind the
facts of history. In an era that strives for
knowledge according to standards set by science,
much of Toynbee's history was rooted in poetry and
prophecy. In a secular age, he saw religion as the
principal goal of life and the essential concern of
the historian. Although he disclaimed the role of
prophet, like the ancient Hebrew prophets, Toynbee,
in a time of social distress and moral confusion,
exhorted man to find certainty in God's ethical
precepts. Like them he warned that when man for-
gets God and worships human creations he brings
disaster upon himself and the social order. Such
an outlook was most certain to arouse criticism.

TOYNBEE AND THE TRADITION OF LIBERAL HUMANISM

Historians have assailed Toynbee as an enemy
of the liberal-rational tradition and have accused
him of advocating and welcoming the decline of the
West. H. R. Trevor-Roper held that Toynbee "is
fundamentally anti-rational and illiberal. Everything which suggests the freedom of the human reason, the human spirit, is to him odious. ... To
Toynbee the Renaissance was the beginning of the
irreversible decline of the West, and every further
manifestation of human reason is to him yet another
milestone on the road to ruin."[1] Toynbee's "dismal
prophecies" that the West was in decline, said
Trevor-Roper, contributed to the spirit of defeatism
with which Western countries first confronted Hitler
in the 1930's. Trevor-Roper attributed to Toynbee
an eagerness to see the West destroyed and for this
reason was "even in 1939 ... blind or indifferent,

to the particular threat of Nazi Germany."[2] Because Toynbee "hungers spiritually" for the defeat of the West and "seems to ... gloat over the extinction of our civilization," Trevor-Roper found his work "hateful."[3] Toynbee would sacrifice Western ideals of justice and freedom, Western rationalism, Western art and literature so long as Christianity, or at least its Catholic strand, survives as part of a syncretic religion of a universal state.

> Why should not our Western Civilization go to its doom, the sooner the better, carrying with it the rubbish with which human reason has by now fatally deformed it, provided that the valuable parts of it, its primitive pre-Reformation faith, can be preserved as one of the vitalizing ingredients of the new 'universal state'?
> ....
> Thus Toynbee is still the philosophic ally of any conqueror who will destroy the West. ... Such, I believe, is Toynbee's philosophy. It is a doctrine of messianic defeatism. Toynbee detests Western Civilization because it is basically liberal and rational. Detesting it, he wishes to see it destroyed, and he does not care who destroys it. On its ruins he envisages a new society, or rather the religion only of a new society. The new society itself, as far as he is concerned, can be the nightmare society of 1984, provided that the religion is the religion of Mish-Mash, of which he is the prophet and Messiah. And this he calls a great hope for the West.[4]

Pieter Geyl expressed somewhat similar sentiments. Toynbee "will have it that Western Civilization is in a bad way, and indeed, why should he care? Western Civilization means nothing to him."[5] Geyl dismissed Toynbee's assurances that he

believes in free will and considers the future
an open question. This assertion, insisted Geyl,
is as invalid as Toynbee's other often repeated
claim that his generalizations derive from an empirical study. By holding that only a return to
Christianity can save the West, an unlikely and un-
satisfying remedy indeed, said Geyl, Toynbee is
condemning all our efforts to futility; it is, in
reality, a death sentence. Despite his criticism
of Spengler, declared Geyl, an exacting determinism pervades Toynbee's system.

These early indictments by Trevor-Roper, Geyl
and many others have been echoed by more recent
critics. In 1968, Sidney Pollard concluded:

> Basically, Toynbee is opposed to
> rationalism. ... Toynbee is instinc-
> tively opposed to all that liberalism
> stands for: freedom to differ, a
> pluralist society, suspicion of
> authority, a belief in the values of
> this life, pursued by rational means,
> within ethical concepts justifiable
> on human rather than mythological or
> divine terms. Toynbee, on the con-
> trary, prefers feeling and intuition
> to analysis; a monolithic God to a
> pluralistic society; fixed, chartered
> course to chance or human initiative;
> and a miracle to partial, piecemeal
> reform.[6]

There is evidence to substantiate the view
that Toynbee was fundamentally hostile to the liberal-rational tradition of the West. His methodology belied the empiricism he claimed for it. By
imposing mythical conceptions of sin, *hubris*, and
Fate upon the course of historical events, Toynbee,
at times, seemed more a prophet or a mystic than
a sober-minded historian. Furthermore, Toynbee
barely acknowledged the accomplishments and the
worth of either Greek humanism or the Enlightenment
tradition. He rejected a secular definition of
freedom, insisted that reason, unguided by spiritual
values, has failed Western man, and stressed

communion with God as the prime aim of life. He
praised the Middle Ages for striking a proper balance between religion and secularism and regarded
modern Western Civilization as a vain repetition of
a disintegrated Hellenic civilization. Like other
twentieth-century intellectuals, Toynbee expressed
a disillusionment with the Enlightenment conception
of man and society. Even when the humanist creed
encompasses non-religious spiritual values, as was
the case with the philosophes, it will not succeed.

It can be argued that a pessimistic if not a
defeatist attitude pervades Toynbee's thought. To
be sure he denied that the West is doomed by necessity and insisted that man is free to shape his
future. Yet he paraded before us dead and dying
civilizations, none of which had succeeded in escap-
ing from the cycle of breakdown and disintegration.
Nor did he think that our modern Western Civilization is worth very much; it is just another meaningless repetition of the Gentiles. If an apostasy
from Christianity has caused our decline and only
allegiance to a revitalized Christianity or a new
syncretic religion can reverse the process of decline, then indeed there is little hope for us.

And yet this view requires qualification and
clarification. Toynbee tried to resolve a fundamental dilemma of the West -- finding a constructive place for the non-rational in a world that is
being increasingly rationalized. For this reason,
he rebelled against the reductionism inherent in
the Enlightenment conception of reason; he wanted
to rescue personality and feelings from reason
which, in its relentless drive to make everything
intelligible, degenerates into soulless mechanism,
materialism, and technocracy. He held that reason
is insufficient to protect man from himself; it is
no match for individual self-centeredness and group
tribal-mindedness that evoke the brutal side of
human nature. It cannot compare with religion in
awakening man's noblest sentiments -- love and compassion. Enlightenment values unbutressed by
Christianity cannot restrain man's basest impulses
nor contain the explosive energies of the non-
rational. Liberalism divested of Christian love

degenerates into greed and competiveness that promote social injustice and the plundering of nature.
Nor can a purely secular statement of liberty safe-
guard individual rights against the claims of the
state; only when personal freedom is conceived as
God's intention for humanity will man have the
spiritual strength to resist totalitarianism. Because the ideals of the Enlightenment and of liberalism were divested of Christian spirituality, they
have failed and will continue to fail Western man.
Secular humanism, insisted Toynbee, is not sufficient by itself. It failed in Periclean Athens,
Medicean Florence, and Victorian England. It was
out of a concern for human dignity which has been
threatened by technology and totalitarianism that
Toynbee urged man to revitalize prophetic values.
When scientists and statesmen become inspired by
spiritual values, reason will be an instrument for
human betterment. Reason requires a spiritual ally,
otherwise all efforts at reform will be defeated by
human self-centeredness and all efforts to undo the
dehumanizing excesses of reason will fail.

But Toynbee was no enemy of reason. He was no
Nietzsche or Sorel glorifying primitive feelings.
What else was his hostility to nationalism and fanaticism but a recognition of the dangers of the
non-rational and a desire to control it? In recognizing and condemning the failings of institutional
religion and in refusing to accept dogma as truth,
Toynbee showed that he was not a simple-minded be-
liever or an obscurantist seeking security in the
orthodoxy of the Middle Ages. Nor did he negate
this world for an afterlife or espouse the with-
drawal from the worldly life. He declared that
Christianity had erred grievously when it fought
the Copernican Revolution with theological doctrines derived essentially from Hellenistic thought
which had nothing at all to do with the essential
meaning of the religion of Jesus. But if Toynbee
would not deny reason, he was keenly aware of its
limitations.

> I would describe myself as ... a 'trans-
> rationalist'. I believe that one must
> follow reason as far as reason will

carry one, and that the findings
of reason ... must be accepted
without reservation. ... I also
hold, however, that reason has not
explained, and probably never will
explain more than a fragment of
the mystery of the universe, and
that the fragmentary picture that
reason gives has to be supplanted
by intuition. I believe that human beings cannot be without this
wider 'trans-rational' vision. At
the same time, I believe that intuition cannot give the verifiable
and demonstrable knowledge that
reason can legitimately claim to
give within its own limited field.[7]

In his humanitarianism, cosmopolitanism, and
concern for social justice, in his willingness to
accept the conclusions of science, in his insistence that man, through intelligent planning, can
utilize technology to improve the quality of life,
and in his hatred of totalitarianism, Toynbee was
heir to the liberal-rational tradition of the West.
Although he insisted that the values of liberal humanism are insufficient to protect man from fanaticism, irrationalism, and a persistent tribal-
mindedness or to give him the inner strength with
which to confront the anxieties and depressions
that burden every human soul, he nevertheless
sought to preserve much of the liberal-rational
tradition by buttressing it with prophetic teachings.

If by liberal we mean protection of individual rights, the rule of law, legitimate parliamentary government, freedom of thought, toleration,
social justice, then Toynbee must be adjudged a
liberal. "Toynbee *is* in many ways rather typical
liberal-democrat-socialist," concludes Roland
Stromberg. "He wants the welfare state and the
United Nations and racial equality and all the
rest."[8] The anonymous reviewer of the *Times Literary Supplement* was quite correct to describe *A
Study of History* as "a vision which expresses the

116

despair of a liberal who has seen the liberal dream turn to ashes as well as the hopes of a liberal who has turned again to God."[9]

Nor was Toynbee devoid of hope for Western Civilization. He insisted that "we must not be defeatist, passive, or aloof in our reaction to the current evils that threaten mankind's survival. If these evils were caused by forces beyond human control, resignation and submission might be the only course open to us. However, our present evils are man-made and ought to be man-cured as well."[10] Toynbee considered it "shameful, and therefore, demoralizing to allow ourselves to be destroyed by refusing to make an effort that is manifestly within our power and that would manifestly save us if we were willing to make it."[11]

LIMITATIONS

Toynbee was no enemy of reason and freedom and he did not seek the destruction of Western Civilization. Nevertheless, he did blur the essential achievements of the modern West and did champion an orientation that could only weaken the liberal-rational tradition. Toynbee paid scant attention to the immense achievement of the modern West which produced a new approach to the study of nature, legal safeguards for the individual, constitutional government, religious toleration, and intellectual freedom.

> When I ask my fellow Westerners what the West stands for, and am told, as I usually am, that it stands for justice, freedom and humanity, I ask if there is any civilization on record -- not excluding those once represented by the Assyrians and the Aztecs -- that has not also claimed to stand for the self-same virtues. Surely these are the virtues to which all human beings feel themselves constrained to pay homage, but to which no human beings have ever succeeded in living up.[12]

To claim that the idea of freedom is universal is simply poor history and Toynbee should have known better. In creating democratic government the modern West brought to fruition an achievement that had its roots in the Greek polis, medieval representative institutions, the English Revolution of the seventeenth century, the natural rights philosophy of John Locke, and the French Revolution. No such comparable development existed in the East where the idea of political freedom and the institution of parliamentary government were alien. Because democracy was not native to the historical experience of Asia and Africa it has proven to be a fragile transplant. It is because of the spread of Western values that Chinese women no longer have their feet bound, that untouchability was abolished in India, that Muslim women are no longer compelled to wear the veil, that humanity condemns slavery as a violation of human rights, and that the poor of the world no longer regard poverty as their destiny. Only under prodding did Toynbee give recognition to the achievements of the modern West.

It is true that the expectations of the philosophes have not been fulfilled, that Condorcet's vision appears to us as an expression of naive optimism. But reason cannot provide that sense of certainty that derives from faith. What it offers is an independent and objective method of proceeding -- a method that welcomes and benefits from critical analysis and debate and rejects appeals to authority. And it is still this critical exercise of reason in the spirit of the Socratic dialogue that affords man the best means for achieving knowledge and with it self-liberation. Better than anyone Freud understood that against the power of instinctual life the intellect is often a feeble weapon. Yet Freud still urged the life of reason. "The voice of the intellect is a soft one," he wrote, "but it does not rest till it has gained a hearing. Finally, after a countless succession of rebuffs, it succeeds. This is one of the few points on which one may be optimistic about the future of mankind." And the same aims one expects from God, says Freud, "namely the love of man and the decrease of suffering," are the aims that the intellect will set for itself. Thus there may be no ultimate antagonism between the aim of the prophets of higher religions and the aim of Socrates, but "an illusion it would be to suppose that what science cannot give us we can get elsewhere."[13]

By treating history as a theodicy, by drawing inspiration from Augustinian pessimism and Bergsonian mysticism, Toynbee, whatever his intention, weakens respect for *logos* at a time when reason needs all the assistance the intellectual community is capable of providing. If the rational foundations of our civilization are eroded, we are more likely to experience an intensification of political myths that appeal to primitive feelings and a proliferation of irrational behavior patterns than we are to experience a reawakening of prophetic values.

To cope with the crisis of our civilization we shall have to renew our confidence in reason, enlarge our understanding of the non-rational, and affirm our commitment to freedom -- that means building upon the achievement of the Enlightenment. And toward this end the historian has a profound responsibility, even a calling as Toynbee holds. As to the nature of that calling the sentiments of J. H. Plumb seem preferable to those of Toynbee:

> Man's success has derived from his application of reason, whether this has been to technical or to social questions. And it is the duty of the historian to teach this, to proclaim it, to demonstrate it in order to give humanity some confidence in a task that will still be cruel and long -- the resolution of the tensions and antipathies that exist within the human species ... Hence the historian's opportunity is similar, although far from identical, to that of the philosophers of the Enlightenment. They too were slipping off the shackles of the past, destroying its pretensions and its

follies, but they also attempted to
create out of the debris a more extended, a more rational, a more de-
tached sense of human destiny. And
so by his writings, by his thinking,
even by his example, the historian
today should be similarly engaged.[14]

Toynbee's religious orientation does not provide a sound basis for coping with the crises of
the modern West or with the world's problems in
this new age of globalism. Can a spiritual transformation be achieved when Western man's religious
world-view has been shattered, its dogmatic and institutional foundation subverted, when God's very
existence is doubted? Even if religion is socially
useful, even if it relieves psychic distress, can
Western intellectuals, in a mental climate shaped
by science and scepticism, return to what they no
longer accept as true? Can prophetic values un-
supported by the mystery and authority of theology
and the power of an institutional church sustain a
spiritual revolution? Higher religions have survived because the inspiration of their prophets was
transformed and hardened into dogma. Not Jesus'
Sermon on the Mount but the Pauline doctrine of a
resurrected savior-God became the centerpiece of
Christianity and made its triumph possible. A religion of love not rooted in dogma and protected by
priests may inspire sporadic outbreaks of spiritual
idealism but that is all. The religious revolution
that Toynbee seeks -- "a conversion of the soul
away from the World, the Flesh, and the Devil to
the Kingdom of Heaven"[15] -- cannot be achieved
through prophetic love alone, for without mystery
and authority, religion fades. And the modern West
is no longer receptive to the mystery and authority
of Christianity.

In a post-Christian scientific age in which a
religious world-view has crumbled and in which
Christianity has evidenced little ability to recon-
vert Westerners to their ancestral religion, Toynbee's hope for a contemporary St. Francis to lead
wayward Westerners back to the God of love seems an
expression of piety not reality. Perhaps this is

one of the reasons why Toynbee in his later works
seemed increasingly more enamored of Eastern religions. The East, less scientific, industrialized
and secularized, and traditionally more introspec-
tive, might prove more receptive to a religious
revolution than the West. Even if the equation between an accelerating rationalization of nature and
society and a decreasing adherence to traditional
religious beliefs, can be upset, how could a religious reawakening take place? On this point the
judgment of Hans Morganthau seems most perceptive:

> But even if it were true that the re-
> turn to religious faith can save
> Western Civilization, can a civili-
> zation recover its religious faith
> by an act of will? ... Neither a
> teacher nor a whole civilization
> can by an act of will create the
> symbolic and ritualistic expressions
> of religiosity thus restored; least
> of all can they create them out of
> the fragments of religions, whose
> decline has made the restoration of
> religiosity necessary in the first
> place. What religions will grow
> from this new religiosity man must
> leave to fate. He must be content
> to be ready, and to make others ready,
> to see the signs and to read them
> aright when they appear.[16]

Toynbee's vision of the harmonization of the
world's higher religions also seems doubtful, for
it is based on the questionable assumption that
these religions are spiritually equivalent, that
their common concern for a higher reality outweighs
disparities resulting from theological differences
and separate histories. This is not the sober
judgment of a historian but the faith of a mystic.

Toynbee also held out the possibility that
twentieth-century man's "quest for the recovery of
religion" may lead to new forms of religion "that
will be so different from the traditional forms
that, at first sight, man's new religion may hardly

be recognizable."[17] The very formlessness of Toynbee's religion of the future opens the door to all forms of religious expression from futile mysticism to violent eruptions of the non-rational, the very thing that Toynbee was trying to guard against. A religious revolution that calls for a return to spiritual values but offers no institutional structure, no theology can degenerate into recklessness, mindlessness, or even self-destruction; or it can remain ineffectual.

There is also the reverse danger. A reawakening of religion might lead not to a heightening of prophetic values but an intensification of fundamentalist dogmatism. Where this has occurred, particularly in the Islamic world, it has been accompanied by a reactionary social policy and an intensification of nationalism. Embracing a religious frame of reference encompasses more than prophetic values; it also invites the authority of priests and the mystery of dogma. This is not what Toynbee desired but it is certainly one of the lessons of history. Nor does religion fulfill the expectations of its prophets. It promises ultimate knowledge and a way of living that is on the highest ethical plane. "Yet its effect is the very opposite," says Ernst Cassirer. "In its concrete appearance it becomes the source of the most profound dissensions and fanatic struggles among men. Religion claims to be in possession of an absolute truth, but its history is a history of errors and heresies. It gives us the promise and prospect of a transcendent world -- far beyond the limits of our human experience -- and it remains, all too human."[18] Thus the heightening of religious feeling might well serve to impede the world-mindedness that Toynbee sought, exacerbate the nationalism that he hated, and thwart the social progress that he advocated.

Religion can do many things, some of them inspiring of awe, but by its very nature it cannot objectively and self-critically analyze and resolve the problems of the human community. To the Socratic quest for knowledge of man, religion offers no rational explanations; it does not clarify the mystery of man but relates a story of sin and salvation that transcends objective knowledge. It must always take as its source and inspiration a standard that emanates from a higher realm and must always conceive this standard as ultimate truth whether or not it is a fruitful guide for intellectual enlightenment or social reconstruction.

The growing world integration in the modern era has not been the creation of religions but of business, science, and technology and it is doubtful that a religious revival will accelerate world-mindedness. Fundamentalist Hindus, Muslims, and Christians have less in common than scientists and technicians whatever their nationality. Science speaks a language of universal reason; while higher religions undoubtedly hold the ideal of universalism, they nevertheless are rooted in the concrete historical experience of a particular civilization. As such they might be a barrier rather than an aid to world unity.

THE ACHIEVEMENT

Of what value is Toynbee's immense effort? Will future generations admire *A Study of History* or will it only "be a curiosity in 20 or 30 years,"[19] as Bruce Mazlish suggested? Toynbee's work will always remain a profound expression of the torments and anxieties that have afflicted the West in the twentieth century. Future historians will also praise *A Study of History* for its innumerable stimulating and illuminating insights, for its wealth of data and extraordinary learning. Toynbee deserves credit for attempting a universal history, for stressing the value of all the world's civilizations and for eschewing Western ethnocentrism. If our planet does become increasingly unified then Toynbee will be heralded as a leading prophet and apostle of world unity. "To have stressed ... the fundamental oneness of mankind," says Hans Kohn, "will be a lasting merit of Mr. Toynbee's work and vision."[20]

Toynbee also deserves praise for daring to take a panoramic view of history in an age when historians are reluctant to venture outside their specializations. William H. McNeill is correct in holding "that there are insights attainable by taking large views of the past which cannot be had from close inspection of separated segments of history. ... It is passages,... when the free exercise of a synthetic imagination has succeeded in suggesting novel relationships and discerning new points of view, which ... make Toynbee a truly great historian."[21] There will always remain a need for historians to produce a comprehensive statement that attempts to give meaning to the many disparate elements that constitute human history in general and Western history in particular.

Perhaps the principal value of Toynbee's effort is that it forces us to reexamine the nature and central meaning of the Enlightenment tradition and to recognize the importance and enduring power of the non-rational in human affairs. Toynbee will ever remind us that theoretical reason, the great achievement of the Greek mind, is not the only component of Western Civilization; there is also the Christian tradition. For Socrates, knowing oneself meant that man's reason and will were autonomous; the human mind did not depend on forces outside itself for defining values and guiding conduct. Christianity represents an alternate and essentially opposing world-view. It teaches that man through reason alone cannot arrive at moral standards and cannot fully know himself, that the cause of sin, suffering, and sorrow is man's separation from God, that man cannot without God's grace overcome his sinful nature, and that the cure for an ailing humanity is communion with God. To regard this anthropology as ignorance or superstition is to misunderstand entirely the persistence and granite might of the non-rational, the well-spring of religious thought. Human nature will resist the complete rationalization of life; it will not discard every mythical explanation or reduce all belief to objective knowledge. To expect it to do otherwise is to misread the historical record and to oversimplify man's being.

The withering of traditional religion has not

meant the complete triumph of reason, the victory of *logos* over *mythos*. Surely the experience of the twentieth century teaches us that the vitality of myth endures, that when man ceases to believe in God he is capable of believing in anything and everything else. Herein lies the ultimate significance of Toynbee's effort. He forces us to confront the irrational, to find a constructive outlet for its creative energies and to cope with its destructive capacities. Who could deny his insight that man's religious sentiments have not been eradicated but have been rerouted into lower religions: the cult of the state, the cult of the race, the cult of the leader, the cult of the party, the cult of the machine? The non-rational is a permanent component of human nature that reason cannot obliterate; the human psyche will not submit to the total ratiocination of life. It is an axiom of Toynbee's thought that if man is deprived of higher religions that stress love and compassion he will embrace lower religions and dangerous myths whose capacity to destroy civilization has been historically demonstrated. On this point we have no assurance that Toynbee is mistaken. Toynbee compels us to consider if the source of evil is not within man himself, if human nature is not indeed afflicted with a vein of wickedness and aggressiveness, what religious thinkers call original sin. Toynbee agrees with Walter Lipmann that "men have been barbarians much longer than they have been civilized. They are only precariously civilized, and within us there is the propensity, persistent as the force of gravity, to revert under stress and strain, under neglect or temptation, to our first natures."[22]

Toynbee reminds us that religion is not something that we can simply reason away and forces us to reflect upon the meaning and utility of prophetic teachings for a secular but troubled age. By questioning the assumption that traditional liberal humanism offers the best defense against dangerous eruptions of the non-rational, Toynbee forces the humanist to reexamine, modify, and improve the instruments of reason.

Toynbee prods us to ask where is science

taking us and cautions us that our technical society, in the words of Jacques Ellul, manifests a
"raving rationalism." Faustian man in his determi-
nation to pursue truth and subdue nature, has
shaped an artificial world of imagined needs, a
Frankenstein technology and giant bureaucracies
that can depersonalize him and destroy the planet.
Like early nineteenth-century romantics, Toynbee
criticizes technicians for turning flesh-and-blood
man into a soulless thinking machine and a vibrant
nature into lifeless wheels, cogs, and pulleys.
Like adherents of eastern religions, he attacks
Westerners for their irreverent attitude toward
nature. By regarding nature as something that God
has given man to exploit, Westerners have plundered
and polluted the planet. Man can only survive,
says Toynbee, if he restrains greed, practices fru-
gality, and adopts a religious reverence for life
and nature.

Toynbee demands that we find meaning in what
many consider a meaningless universe, and cautions
us that science alone cannot provide this meaning,
cannot grasp life in its fullness. He warns us
that the bedrock of civilization is not man's domin-
ion over nature but the moral mastery of his own
nature and the quality of his relations with his
fellows. The ills of modern society, he insists,
cannot be cured merely by organizational or institutional changes. Mankind requires a change of
heart, a better spiritual orientation. To a stum-
bling Western Civilization he warns further that
civilizations break down from within, from a failure of leadership and a loss of élan. If a civilization is to endure it must be directed toward
something more inspiring than material gain. And
he admonishes those who would surrender to despair:
"We must strive to win the battle of life though we
have no guarantee that we will."[23]

Toynbee is more poet and artist than social
scientist. But his very subjectivity accounts for
his achievement. Many of the questions he asks are
not capable of empirical verification, but they do
awaken the historical imagination and provoke philosophic discourse. In an age that has seen reason

and optimism soar and collapse, Toynbee has raised the essential questions.

NOTES

1. H. R. Trevor-Roper, *Historical Essays*, pp. 300-01.

2. *Ibid.*, p. 305.

3. *Ibid.*, pp. 320-21.

4. *Ibid.*, pp. 309, 322-23.

5. Pieter Geyl, *Debates with Historians*, p. 185.

6. Sidney Pollard, *The Idea of Progress* (London: C.A. Watts & Co., 1968), p. 173.

7. Arnold J. Toynbee, "The Future of Religion," *Twentieth Century* 17 (Autumn 1961), p. 114.

8. Roland N. Stromberg, *Arnold Toynbee Historian for an Age of Crisis* (Carbondale, Illinois: Southern Illinois University Press, 1972), p. 82.

9. Montagu, ed., *Toynbee and History*, p. 110.

10. *The Toynbee - Ikeda Dialogue* (New York: Kodansha International Ltd., 1976), p. 55.

11. *Ibid.*, p. 57.

12. *Study*, 12: 626-27.

13. Sigmund Freud, *The Future of an Illusion*, trans. W. D. Robson-Scott, revised and newly edited by James Strachey (Garden City, New York: Doubleday Anchor Books, 1964), pp. 87-88, 90.

14. J. H. Plumb, *The Death of the Past* (Boston: Houghton Mifflin Co., 1970), pp. 142, 144-45.

15. *Study*, 3: 192.

16. Hans J. Morganthau, "Toynbee and the Historical Imagination," in Montagu, ed., *Toynbee and History*, pp. 198-99.

17. Arnold J. Toynbee, "The Challenge of Our Era," in *New Frontiers of Knowledge*, a symposium by distinguished writers, notable scholars, and public figures (Washington, D. C.: Public Affairs Press, 1957), P. 24.

18. Ernst Cassirer, *An Essay on Man* (New York: Bantam Books, 1970), pp. 79-80.

19. Bruce Mazlish, *The Riddle of History: The Great Speculators from Vico to Freud* (New York: Minerva Press, 1968), p. 368.

20. Kohn, *Political Ideologies of the Twentieth Century*, p. 275.

21. Gargan, ed., *The Intent of Toynbee's History*, pp. 30, 41.

22. Walter Lippmann, *The Public Philosophy* (Boston: Little, Brown and Co., 1955), p. 86.

23. *The Toynbee-Ikeda Dialogue*, p. 75.

BIBLIOGRAPHY

A complete listing of Toynbee's works and the
secondary literature would cover scores of pages.
A useful bibliography of Toynbee's writings is
Monica Popper, *A Bibliography of the Works in English of Arnold Toynbee 1910-1954* (London: Royal
Institute of International Affairs, 1955).   A listing of works about Toynbee is found in John C. Rule
and Barbara S. Crosby, "Bibliography of Works about
Toynbee in Western Languages, 1946-1960," *History
and Theory* 4 (1964):   213-33.   Toynbee himself in
volume 12 of *A Study of History* has compiled a
bibliography of most of the reviews and articles
dealing with his project.   A recent and complete
bibliography of both Toynbee's writings and critical secondary works is S. Fiona Morton, *A Bibliography of Arnold J. Toynbee* (New York: Oxford
University Press), 1981.

SELECTED WORKS OF ARNOLD TOYNBEE

Toynbee, Arnold J. *A Study of History.*   12 vols.   New York:
Oxford University Press, 1934-1961.   Oxford University
Press has also published the paperback edition.   A
two-volume abridgement of volumes 1-10 was prepared by
D. C. Somervell and published by Oxford University
Press, 1947, 1957.   There is also an abridged, illus-
trated, one-volume edition published jointly by Oxford
University Press and American Heritage Press, 1972.

_____. *Survey of International Affairs.*   London: Oxford
University Press.   Issued under the auspices of the
Royal Institute of International Affairs.   Toynbee was
wholly or partly responsible for most of the volumes
covering the period 1920-1950.

_____. "The Issue in British Foreign Policy." *Inter-
national Affairs* 17 (May-June 1938):   307-337.

_____. "After Munich: The World Outlook." *Interna-
tional Affairs* 18 (January-February 1939):   1-28.

_____. "A Turning Point in History." *Foreign Affairs*
17 (January 1939):   305-320.

_____. *Civilization on Trial.*   New York: Oxford

University Press, 1948.

_____. *The Prospects of Western Civilization*. New York: Columbia University Press, 1949.

_____. *The World and the West*. New York: Oxford University Press, 1953.

_____. *A Study of History, What the Book is For: How the Book Took Shape*. New York: Oxford University Press, 1954.

_____. *An Historian's Approach to Religion*. New York: Oxford University Press, 1956.

_____. *Christianity Among the Religions of the World*. New York: Charles Scribner's Sons, 1957.

_____. *Democracy in the Atomic Age*. New York: Oxford University Press, 1957.

_____. "The Writing of History." *Times Literary Supplement*, August 15, 1958. Special issue entitled "Books in a Changing World."

_____. *East to West*. New York: Oxford University Press, 1958.

_____. *Hellenism*. New York: Oxford University Press, 1959.

_____. "The Future of Religion." *Twentieth Century* 170 (Autumn 1961): 114-39.

_____. *Between Oxus and Jumna*. New York: Oxford University Press, 1961.

_____. *America and the World Revolution and Other Lectures*. New York: Oxford University Press, 1962.

_____. and Toynbee, Phillip. *Comparing Notes: A Dialogue Across a Generation*. London: Weidenfeld & Nicolson, 1963.

_____. *Janus at 75*. New York: Oxford University Press, 1964.

_____. *Between Niger and Nile.* New York: Oxford University Press, 1965.

_____. *Change and Habit.* New York: Oxford University Press, 1966.

_____. *Between Maule and Amazon.* New York: Oxford University Press, 1967.

_____. *Acquaintances.* New York: Oxford University Press, 1967.

_____. "A Substitute for War?" *Long Island Press,* 3 May, 1969, p. 13.

_____. *Experiences.* New York: Oxford University Press, 1969.

_____. *Cities on the Move.* New York: Oxford University Press, 1970.

_____. *Surviving the Future.* New York: Oxford University Press, 1971.

_____. "For the First Time in 30,000 Years." *Worldview* 15 (March 1972): 5-9.

_____. *Mankind and Mother Earth.* New York: Oxford University Press, 1976.

WORKS WHICH TOYNBEE CONTRIBUTED TO OR EDITED

Livingstone, Richard, ed. *The Legacy of Greece.* London: Clarendon Press, 1921; reprint ed. New York: Oxford University Press, Galaxy, 1969.

Toynbee, Arnold, et. al. *Frontiers of Knowledge.* A Symposium by Distinguished Writers, Notable Scholars, and Public Figures. Washington, D.C.: Public Affairs Press, 1957.

Meyers, Edward D. *Education in the Perspective of History.* New York: Harper & Row, 1960. A concluding chapter by Toynbee.

Toynbee, Arnold, ed. *Cities of Destiny.* New York: McGraw Hill, 1967.

Toynbee, Arnold, et. al. *The Impact of the Russian Revolution 1917-1967*. New York: Oxford University Press, 1967.

Toynbee, Arnold, et. al. *Man's Concern with Death*. London: Hudder and Stoughton, 1968.

Toynbee, Arnold, ed. *The Crucible of Christianity*. New York: World Publishing Co., 1969.

Ng, Larry, ed. *Alternatives to Violence*. New York: Time-Life Books, 1968.

SELECTED WORKS ON ARNOLD TOYNBEE

Africa, Thomas W. "The City of God Revisited: Toynbee's Reconsiderations," *Journal of History of Ideas* 23 (April 1, 1962): 282-92.

Aron, Raymond, ed. *L'histoire et ses interpretations: entretiens autour de Arnold Toynbee*. Paris: Mouton, 1961.

Brinton, Crane. "Toynbee's City of God." *Virginia Quarterly Review* 32 (Summer 1956): 361-75.

Christian, James Lee. "Arnold Toynbee's Concept of Man." Ph.D. dissertation. Boston University, 1957.

Collingwood, R. G. *The Idea of History*. New York: Oxford University Press, 1946.

D'Arcy, M. C. *The Meaning and Matter of History*. New York: Noonday Press, 1967.

Dawson, Christopher. *The Dynamics of World History*. New York: Sheen & Ward, 1956; reprint ed., New York: Mentor, 1962.

Donagan, Alan and Donagan, Barbara. *Philosophy of History*. New York: MacMillan, 1965.

Engel-Janosi, Friedrich. "Toynbee and the Tradition of Universal History, A Sketch." The McAuley Lectures, 1957. Saint Joseph College, West Hartford, Conn., 1957, pp. 221-47.

Frankel, Charles. *The Case for Modern Man.* New York: Harper & Row, 1955.

Gargan, Edward T., ed. *The Intent of Toynbee's History.* Chicago: Loyola University Press, 1961.

Geyl, Pieter, Toynbee, Arnold, and Sorokin, Pitrim. *The Pattern of the Past: Can We Determine It?* Boston: Beacon Press, 1949.

Geyl, Pieter. *Debates With Historians.* New York: Philosophical Library, 1956.

Hill, Christopher. "Dr. Toynbee's SNARK." *Spectator* 206 (May 12, 1961): 685.

Hunnex, Milton deVerne. "Toynbee's Idea of Etheralization as a Criterion of Progress." Ph.D. dissertation. University of Redlands, 1957.

Kahler, Erich. *The Meaning of History.* New York: George Braziller, 1964; reprint ed., Cleveland: World Publishing Co., Meridean, 1968.

Kirkwood, Kenneth P. "Arnold J. Toynbee Philosopher of History." An Address Given at the British Council. Karachi, March 1953.

Kohn, Hans. *Political Ideologies of the Twentieth Century.* 3d ed. New York: Harper Torchbooks, 1966.

Manuel, Frank E. *Shapes of Philosophical History.* Stanford, California: Stanford University Press, 1965.

Martin, Percival W. *Experiment in Depth: A Study of the Work of Jung, Eliot and Toynbee.* London: Routledge, 1955.

Mason, Henry L. *Toynbee's Approach to World Politics.* New Orleans: Tulane University Press, 1958.

Mazlish, Bruce. *The Riddle of History.* New York: Harper & Row, 1966; reprint ed. New York: Minerva Press, 1968.

Melko, Matthew. *The Nature of Civilizations.* Boston: Porter Sargent, 1969.

133

Montagu, M. R. Ashley, ed. *Toynbee and History*. Boston: Porter Sargent, 1956.

Nash, Ronald, ed. *Ideas of History*. 2 vols. New York: E. P. Dutton, 1969.

Perry, Marvin. "Arnold Toynbee: Nationalism as a False God." *Interpretation: A Journal of Political Philosophy* 4 (1974): 48-62.

Perry, Marvin. "Legacy of Arnold Toynbee." *Commonweal* 102 (December 19, 1975): 630-31.

Pollard, Sidney. *The Idea of Progress*. London: C. A. Watts & Co., 1968.

Stromberg, Roland N. *Arnold J. Toynbee Historian For An Age of Crisis*. Carbondale, Illinois: Southern Illinois University Press, 1972.

Sullivan, Richard E. "Toynbee's Debtors." *South Atlantic Quarterly* 58 (Winter 1959): 77-90.

Thompson, Kenneth W. "Toynbee and World Politics: Democracy and Foreign Policy." *The Review of Politics* 18 (October 1956): 418-43.

Trevor-Roper, H. R. "Arnold Toynbee's Millenium." *Encounter* 8 (June 1957): 14-28; reprinted in *Historical Essays*. New York: Harper Torchbooks, 1966.

Wagar, W. Warren. *The City of Man*. Boston: Houghton Mifflin, 1967; reprint ed. Baltimore: Penquin, 1963.

_____. *Good Tidings: The Belief in Progress From Darwin to Marcuse*. Bloomington, Indiana: Indiana University Press, 1972.

White, Hayden V. "Collingwood and Toynbee: Transitions in English Historical Thought." *English Miscellany*. Rome, 1957, pp. 147-178.

Woodward, C. Vann. "Toynbee and Metahistory." *The American Scholar* 27 (Summer 1958): 384-92.